# THE ULTIMATE STOCK MARKET PLAY BOOK

## Strategies For Building Long-Term Wealth

GRAHAM STERLING

# The Ultimate Stock Market Play Book

Copyright © 2024 by Graham Sterling]

All rights reserved. No part of this book may be reproduced, distributed, or transmitted in any form or by any means, including photocopying, recording, or other electronic or mechanical methods, without the prior written permission of the publisher, except in the case of brief quotations embodied in critical reviews and certain other noncommercial uses permitted by copyright law.

# TABLE OF CONTENT

INTRODUCTION ........................................................... 7
   The Ultimate Stock Market Playbook ......... 7
   Why the Stock Market Matters ..................... 7
   Myths and Realities About Investing ........... 8
   Setting Your Financial Goals ....................... 10
   How to Use This Playbook ........................... 10
   Who This Book is For .................................... 11
   A Glimpse into the Journey Ahead ............ 12

Part 1: The Foundations of Stock Market Investing ............................................................... 14

Chapter 1 ...................................................................... 14
   Understanding the Stock Market ................ 14

Chapter 2 ...................................................................... 25
   Essential Stock Market Terms ..................... 25

Chapter 3 ...................................................................... 35
   The Psychology of Investing ........................ 35

Part 2: Developing a Winning Strategy ........ 44

Chapter 4 ...................................................................... 44
   Setting Clear Investment Goals .................. 44

Chapter 5 ...................................................................... 53
   Building a Strong Portfolio ............................ 53

Chapter 6 ...................................................................... 63

Stock Research and Analysis ..... 63

Fundamental Analysis: ..... 63

Chapter 7 ..... 72

Timing the Market vs. Time in the Market 72

Debunking Market Timing Myths ..... 72

Part 3: Practical Investing Techniques ..... 80

Chapter 8 ..... 80

Getting Started with Your First Investment ..... 80

Choosing a Brokerage Platform ..... 80

Chapter 9 ..... 90

Dividend Investing for Steady Income ..... 90

Understanding Dividend Investing ..... 90

Chapter 10 ..... 100

Growth Investing Strategies ..... 100

What is Growth Investing? ..... 100

Chapter 11 ..... 110

Value Investing ..... 110

What is Value Investing? ..... 110

Part 4: Managing and Growing Your Investments ..... 119

Chapter 12 ..... 119

Monitoring and Adjusting Your Portfolio 119

1. Regularly Review Your Portfolio's Performance ... 120

Chapter 13 ... 130

Tax Implications of Investing ... 130

Chapter 14 ... 139

Mitigating Risks in Investing ... 139

1. Stop-Loss Orders and Other Protective Strategies ... 139

Part 5: Advanced Strategies for Experienced Investors ... 149

Chapter 15 ... 149

Options and Derivatives ... 149

Chapter 16 ... 160

Short Selling Explained ... 160

Chapter 17 ... 171

Sector and Thematic Investing ... 171

Chapter 18 ... 184

The Power of Compounding: Maximizing Long-Term Returns and Real-Life Success Stories ... 184

Chapter 19 ... 195

Lessons from Successful Investors:

Case Studies of Market Titans and Key Takeaways for Individual Investors......195

Chapter 20......204

Creating a Legacy Through, Investing: Passing Wealth to the Next Generation and the Role of Philanthropy in Financial Planning......204

Conclusion......213

Your Ultimate Stock Market Playbook in Action......213

The Foundations of Investing......213

Developing a Winning Strategy......214

Managing and Growing Your Investments 214

Advanced Strategies......214

Legacy Building and Philanthropy......215

Appendices......218

A. Stock Market Resources and Tools 218

1. How Do I Start Investing in the Stock Market?......221

# INTRODUCTION

### The Ultimate Stock Market Playbook

The stock market is a realm of boundless opportunities and unrelenting challenges. It is a space where fortunes are built, dreams are realized, and, at times, mistakes become life lessons. For centuries, the stock market has been a cornerstone of wealth creation, offering individuals and institutions the ability to grow their finances, secure their futures, and contribute to the global economy. Yet, for many, the stock market remains a confusing and intimidating frontier

This playbook is designed to change that narrative. Whether you're a novice taking your first steps or an experienced investor looking to refine your strategies, this book will serve as your ultimate guide to navigating the complexities of the stock market with confidence and clarity.

### Why the Stock Market Matters

The Role of the Stock Market in Wealth Building

The stock market isn't just a place where shares of companies are traded. It's a dynamic ecosystem that powers economic growth, fuels innovation, and allows individuals to participate in the success of global industries. Investing in the stock market gives you the opportunity to become a shareholder in some of the world's most influential companies.

Historically, the stock market has delivered higher returns over the long term compared to other asset classes like bonds or real estate. For instance, the average annual return of the S&P 500 index has been around 10% since its inception. This compounding growth can transform modest investments into substantial wealth over time, making the stock market a key instrument in achieving financial independence.

Consider this: if you invested $10,000 in the S&P 500 in 1990, your investment would be worth over $100,000 today. That is the power of compounding returns—a phenomenon Albert Einstein once referred to as the "eighth wonder of the world."

### *Myths and Realities About Investing*

The stock market often evokes a mix of excitement and apprehension. Unfortunately, much of the fear and confusion surrounding it stems from pervasive myths. Let's debunk some of these misconceptions:

**Myth:** Investing is Gambling

**Reality:** Unlike gambling, which relies on chance, investing is a strategic endeavor based on analysis, research, and informed decision-making. While risks exist, they can be mitigated through diversification, asset allocation, and a disciplined approach.

Myth: You Need a Lot of Money to Invest

Reality: Today, investing is more accessible than ever. With fractional shares and apps that allow micro-investing, you can start with as little as $5.

Myth: Only Experts Can Make Money in the Market

Reality: While expertise helps, success in the stock market is achievable for anyone willing to learn and apply sound principles. This playbook equips you with the knowledge to invest like a pro.

Myth: The Market is Rigged Against Small Investors

Reality: While institutional investors have advantages, retail investors can level the playing field by focusing on long-term strategies and avoiding speculative traps.

Understanding these myths and realities is the first step toward developing a confident, informed approach to investing.

## *Setting Your Financial Goals*

Successful investing begins with a clear vision of your financial goals. Ask yourself:

Are you investing to build a retirement nest egg?

Are you saving for a major life event, like buying a home or funding a child's education?

Do you want to generate passive income or grow your wealth over time?

By defining your objectives, you can tailor your investment strategy to meet your unique needs. Goals act as your roadmap, guiding every decision you make in the market. This playbook will teach you how to align your portfolio with your aspirations, ensuring that every trade or investment is a step toward your desired future.

## How to Use This Playbook
### Overview of Key Concepts and Strategies

The Ultimate Stock Market Playbook is not just another guide to investing. It's a comprehensive manual designed to simplify complex topics, provide actionable strategies, and empower you to take control of your financial destiny.

**Here's what you can expect:**

**Step-by-Step Guidance:** From understanding market basics to mastering advanced strategies, this playbook breaks down every concept in easy-to-understand language.

**Actionable Advice:** Each chapter includes practical tips and tools you can apply immediately to your investment journey.

**Real-Life Examples:** Case studies and anecdotes illustrate key principles, making them relatable and easier to grasp.

**Focus on Long-Term Success:** While short-term gains are enticing, this book emphasizes sustainable wealth-building strategies for lasting financial security.

## Who This Book is For

This playbook is for everyone, regardless of their experience level or financial background:

**Beginners:** If you're new to investing, this book provides a solid foundation to help you get started. You'll learn the basics, avoid common pitfalls, and gain the confidence to make your first investment.

**Intermediate Investors:** If you've been dabbling in the market but lack a cohesive strategy, this playbook will help you refine your approach and achieve consistent results.

**Experienced Investors:** Even seasoned market participants will find value in the advanced techniques and insights presented here, enabling them to take their investing to the next level.

Ultimately, this book is for anyone who believes in the power of the stock market to transform lives. Whether your goal is financial freedom, early retirement, or leaving a legacy for future generations, the Ultimate Stock Market Playbook is your guide to making it happen.

### *A Glimpse into the Journey Ahead*

As you turn the pages of this book, you'll embark on a journey that will demystify the stock market, empower you with knowledge, and equip you with tools to build lasting wealth. You'll learn about the principles of risk management, the psychology of investing, and the strategies that have stood the test of time.

This isn't just a book—it's a blueprint for your financial future. So, grab a pen, take notes, and get ready to rewrite your financial story. Let's turn the stock market from a daunting mystery into a powerful ally on your journey to prosperity.

Welcome to the Ultimate Stock Market Playbook—your guide to achieving your wealth-building dreams.

# Part 1: The Foundations of Stock Market Investing

## Chapter 1

### *Understanding the Stock Market*

The stock market is often described as the beating heart of the global economy. It is a vibrant hub where financial instruments, primarily stocks, are bought and sold, connecting individuals, companies, and economies in a network of wealth creation and value exchange. To truly harness its potential, one must understand its intricacies. This chapter delves deep into what the stock market is, the types of markets, and the key players who drive its operations.

**What Is the Stock Market?**

At its core, the stock market is a marketplace where shares of publicly traded companies are issued, bought, and sold. These shares represent fractional ownership in companies, giving investors the right to a portion of the company's profits and assets.

**The Purpose of the Stock Market**

The stock market serves two primary functions:

**Capital Formation for Companies:**

Companies raise capital by issuing shares through an Initial Public Offering (IPO). This allows them to fund operations, expand business, and invest in new opportunities without taking on debt.

For example, when a company like Apple or Amazon issues stock, it raises money from investors to fuel innovation and growth.

**Investment Opportunities for Individuals:**

For investors, the stock market offers an avenue to grow wealth by purchasing shares that can appreciate in value over time.

Additionally, many stocks pay dividends, providing a regular income stream.

**Stock Exchanges**

The stock market operates through exchanges, which are regulated platforms where securities are traded. Examples include:

**The New York Stock Exchange (NYSE):** Known as the largest and most prestigious exchange globally.

**The NASDAQ:** A tech-heavy exchange that lists companies like Microsoft, Apple, and Tesla.

Other notable exchanges include the London Stock Exchange (LSE), Tokyo Stock Exchange (TSE), and Bombay Stock Exchange (BSE).

Exchanges facilitate transparency, liquidity, and efficiency, ensuring a fair environment for all participants.

**Types of Markets:** Primary vs. Secondary

The stock market is divided into two main segments: the Primary Market and the Secondary Market. Understanding their distinctions is crucial for any investor.

### The Primary Market

The primary market is where securities are created and sold for the first time. It is the stage where companies raise capital by issuing new shares through an IPO.

**Key Features of the Primary Market:**

**Direct Interaction:** Investors purchase shares directly from the issuing company.

**Purpose:** Provides capital to companies to fund growth or repay debt.

**Pricing:** The price of shares in an IPO is determined through underwriting, usually by investment banks.

For instance, when Facebook (now Meta) went public in 2012, it issued shares for the first time in the primary market, raising over $16 billion.

**Other Instruments Traded:** Besides stocks, other securities like bonds and preferred shares can also be issued in the primary market.

**The Secondary Market**

The secondary market is where securities are traded after their initial issuance. Here, investors buy and sell shares among themselves, with no direct involvement of the issuing company. It is the segment most people refer to when discussing the stock market.

Key Features of the Secondary Market:

**Liquidity:** Investors can easily buy and sell shares, converting them into cash or other assets.

**Market Prices:** Prices are determined by supply and demand dynamics, reflecting market sentiment, company performance, and external factors.

**Accessibility:** Unlike the primary market, retail investors have broad access to participate in the secondary market.

For example, when you buy shares of Amazon or Tesla on the NYSE or NASDAQ, you are participating in the secondary market.

**Primary vs. Secondary Market:** A Comparison

| Aspect | Primary Market | Secondary Market |
|---|---|---|
| Purpose | Issuance of new securities | Trading existing securities |
| Participants | Issuing companies and investors | Investors (buyers and sellers) |

Price   Determined by issuing company/underwriters   Determined by market forces (demand/supply)

Role of Issuer  Active (raises capital)  Passive (no direct involvement)

The seamless functioning of both markets is vital for the overall health and efficiency of the stock market ecosystem.

Key Players: Retail Investors, Institutional Investors, and Brokers

The stock market operates through a diverse network of participants, each playing a unique role. Let's examine these key players in detail:

**Retail Investors**

Retail investors are individual investors who buy and sell securities for their personal accounts. They represent the majority of market participants and have varying levels of experience, ranging from beginners to seasoned traders.

**Characteristics of Retail Investors:**

Typically invest smaller amounts compared to institutions.

Use brokerage accounts or trading apps like Robinhood, E*TRADE, or Fidelity.

Driven by personal financial goals such as retirement, education, or wealth building.

### Advantages of Retail Investors:

Can be more flexible and responsive to market trends due to smaller portfolios.

Access to fractional shares allows participation in high-priced stocks like Alphabet or Berkshire Hathaway.

### Challenges for Retail Investors:

Limited resources for research and analysis.

Emotional biases, such as fear and greed, can lead to poor decision-making.

### Institutional Investors

Institutional investors are large organizations, such as mutual funds, hedge funds, pension funds, and insurance companies, that invest significant sums of money on behalf of their clients or members.

### Characteristics of Institutional Investors:

They control a substantial portion of the market's total assets.

Often have access to advanced analytics, research teams, and proprietary trading strategies.

Trades executed by institutions can move markets due to their size.

**Advantages of Institutional Investors:**

Economies of scale allow them to negotiate lower fees and execute trades at better prices.

Professional management ensures strategic allocation of assets.

**Influence on the Market:**

Institutional investors are trendsetters, often determining the direction of the market.

For example, when a major pension fund increases its holdings in a specific stock, it can trigger a rise in demand, leading to price appreciation.

Brokers

Brokers act as intermediaries, connecting buyers and sellers in the stock market. They provide platforms, tools, and services that enable investors to execute trades.

**Types of Brokers:**

**Full-Service Brokers:** Offer personalized advice, research reports, and wealth management services. Examples include Merrill Lynch and Morgan Stanley.

**Discount Brokers:** Provide basic trading services at lower fees, such as Charles Schwab and Interactive Brokers.

**Online Brokers:** Platforms like Robinhood and E*TRADE cater to tech-savvy investors seeking low-cost, user-friendly options.

**Role of Brokers:**

Facilitate market access for retail and institutional investors.

Ensure transparency and compliance with regulatory standards.

Provide analytical tools, educational resources, and customer support to their clients.

**Earning Mechanism:**

Brokers earn through commissions, spreads, or account maintenance fees.

The advent of online trading platforms and

commission-free trades has revolutionized the brokerage industry, making investing more accessible and affordable for retail investors.

**The Interplay Between Key Players**

The stock market thrives on the interaction between retail investors, institutional investors, and brokers. For example:

A retail investor purchases shares of Apple using a brokerage account.

Institutional investors, such as mutual funds, may influence the price through large trades.

Brokers facilitate these transactions, ensuring liquidity and efficient price discovery.

This interconnected ecosystem ensures the smooth functioning of the stock market, allowing individuals and institutions to achieve their financial objectives.

Understanding the stock market, its structure, and its key participants is the foundation for successful investing. By grasping the distinctions between the primary and secondary markets and recognizing the roles of retail investors, institutional investors, and brokers, you gain a clearer picture of how this vast ecosystem operates.

Armed with this knowledge, you are better prepared to navigate the complexities of the market, make informed decisions, and leverage opportunities to achieve your financial goals. The next chapters of this playbook will build on these fundamentals, guiding you toward advanced strategies and tools to maximize your potential in the world of investing.

# Chapter 2

## *Essential Stock Market Terms*

To succeed in the stock market, you need to familiarize yourself with the terminology commonly used in the industry. Understanding these terms not only builds your financial literacy but also empowers you to make informed investment decisions. In this chapter, we'll break down key stock market terms, demystify common jargon, and discuss the various classifications of stocks.

### Market Cap, Dividends, P/E Ratio, and More

These fundamental concepts form the backbone of stock market analysis. Each term provides unique insights into a company's performance, valuation, and potential as an investment.

### Market Capitalization (Market Cap)

Market cap represents the total value of a company's outstanding shares in the market. It is calculated by multiplying the current stock price by the number of outstanding shares.

**Categories of Market Cap:**

**Large-Cap Companies:** Market cap exceeds $10 billion.

Examples: Apple, Microsoft, Amazon.

Stability and lower risk but slower growth.

Mid-Cap Companies: Market cap ranges from $2 billion to $10 billion.

Often in growth phases, offering a balance of risk and reward.

Small-Cap Companies: Market cap is less than $2 billion.

High growth potential but comes with increased volatility.

Market cap is crucial because it helps investors determine a company's size and risk profile, influencing portfolio allocation decisions.

Dividends

Dividends are a portion of a company's profits distributed to shareholders, usually on a quarterly basis.

**Types of Dividends:**

**Cash Dividends:** Paid directly in cash to shareholders.

**Stock Dividends:** Additional shares issued instead of cash.

**Why Dividends Matter:**

Income Source: Ideal for retirees seeking passive income.

**Signal of Financial Health:** Consistent dividends indicate a company's profitability and stability.

Example: Companies like Procter & Gamble and Coca-Cola are known for their reliable dividends, making them popular among income-focused investors.

**Price-to-Earnings (P/E) Ratio**

The P/E ratio measures a company's stock price relative to its earnings per share (EPS). It indicates how much investors are willing to pay for each dollar of earnings.

Formula:

Ratio

=

$$P/E\ Ratio = \frac{\text{Market Price per Share}}{\text{Earnings per Share (EPS)}}$$

**Types of P/E Ratios:**

**High P/E Ratio:** Indicates growth potential but may signal overvaluation.

**Low P/E Ratio:** Suggests undervaluation or a mature company with steady earnings.

Investors use the P/E ratio to compare companies within the same sector and assess valuation.

**Other Key Terms**

**Earnings Per Share (EPS):** Represents the portion of a company's profit allocated to each outstanding share.

Higher EPS indicates greater profitability.

Beta: Measures a stock's volatility relative to the overall market.

A beta greater than 1 implies higher volatility, while less than 1 suggests stability.

Dividend Yield: The annual dividend payment expressed as a percentage of the stock price.

Formula:

$$\text{Dividend Yield} = \frac{\text{Annual Dividend per Share}}{\text{Stock Price}} \times 100$$

$$\text{Dividend Yield} = \frac{\text{Annual Dividend per Share}}{\text{Stock Price}} \times 100$$

Volume: The number of shares traded during a specific period. High volume often signals strong investor interest or significant news.

By mastering these terms, you'll be equipped to interpret financial statements, analyze stocks, and engage in meaningful discussions about investments.

## Common Jargon Every Investor Should Know

The stock market has its own language, and understanding it is essential for navigating the world of investing. Let's explore some of the most common jargon:

### Bull Market vs. Bear Market

Bull Market: A prolonged period of rising stock prices, typically driven by optimism and strong economic performance.

Example: The tech boom of the late 1990s.

**Bear Market:** A sustained decline of 20% or more in stock prices, often reflecting pessimism or economic downturns.

Example: The 2008 financial crisis.

### Blue-Chip Stocks

These are shares of large, established companies with a history of reliability, profitability, and consistent dividends.

Examples: Johnson & Johnson, IBM, and Visa.

IPO (Initial Public Offering)

The process by which a private company becomes publicly traded by offering its shares to the public for the first time.

**Portfolio Diversification**

The practice of spreading investments across various assets to minimize risk.

Example: Holding stocks, bonds, and ETFs in different industries.

By understanding this jargon, you can decode market news, reports, and expert commentary, giving you a significant edge as an investor.

**Types of Stocks**

Not all stocks are created equal. Understanding the different types of stocks helps investors align their portfolio with their financial goals and risk tolerance.

**Common Stocks vs. Preferred Stocks**

**Common Stocks:**

Represent ownership in a company and provide voting rights at shareholder meetings.

Offer potential for capital appreciation and dividends.

Risk: Dividends are not guaranteed and are distributed after bondholders and preferred shareholders.

**Preferred Stocks:**

Provide fixed dividends and priority over common stocks in case of liquidation.

No voting rights, but offer stability and predictable income.

Investors choose between common and preferred stocks based on their risk appetite and income needs.

Growth Stocks, Value Stocks, and Dividend Stocks

**Growth Stocks:**

Belong to companies expected to grow at an above-average rate.

Often reinvest profits into expansion rather than paying dividends.

Examples: Tech companies like Tesla and Amazon.

**Value Stocks:**

Trade at a lower price relative to their fundamentals (e.g., P/E ratio).

Often overlooked but provide significant upside potential.

Example: Berkshire Hathaway.

**Dividend Stocks:**

Offer regular dividend payouts, making them attractive for income-focused investors.

Examples: Verizon, AT&T, and utility companies.

Each type of stock appeals to different investor profiles, and diversification across these categories can optimize a portfolio.

**Sector-Based Classification**

Stocks are also classified based on the sector or industry they belong to:

**Technology:** Companies focused on software, hardware, and IT services.

Examples: Apple, Microsoft, Nvidia.

**Healthcare:** Pharmaceuticals, biotech, and healthcare services.

Examples: Pfizer, Johnson & Johnson.

Financials: Banks, insurance, and investment firms.

Examples: JPMorgan Chase, Goldman Sachs.

**Energy:** Oil, gas, and renewable energy companies.

Examples: ExxonMobil, NextEra Energy.

Understanding sector-based classification helps investors capitalize on industry trends and diversify their holdings effectively.

Mastering essential stock market terms and understanding the various types of stocks is critical for building a strong investment foundation. These concepts allow investors to analyze opportunities, assess risks, and make informed decisions. With this knowledge, you're ready to explore advanced strategies and techniques to maximize your returns and achieve your financial goals.

# Chapter 3

## *The Psychology of Investing*

Successful investing is as much about managing your mindset as it is about analyzing numbers or understanding markets. Emotional decisions, a lack of awareness about risk tolerance, and impatience are among the primary reasons investors fail to achieve their financial goals. This chapter delves into the psychological aspects of investing, emphasizing the need for emotional discipline, understanding your relationship with risk, and fostering patience to navigate the ups and downs of the stock market effectively.

### Avoiding Emotional Decisions

Investing is inherently emotional because money represents security, freedom, and often dreams. However, emotional decision-making can sabotage even the most carefully laid plans. Let's explore why this happens and how to avoid it.

### The Role of Fear and Greed

**Fear:**

Fear of losing money can lead to panic

selling during market downturns.

Example: During the 2008 financial crisis, many investors sold at market lows, locking in losses rather than waiting for recovery.

**Greed:**

The desire for quick profits often results in speculative investments or holding on to overvalued stocks for too long.

Example: The dot-com bubble of the late 1990s saw irrational exuberance, where people ignored fundamentals to chase skyrocketing tech stocks.

## Common Emotional Biases in Investing

**Overconfidence Bias:**

Believing you can consistently "beat the market" leads to excessive risk-taking.

Solution: Stick to a disciplined strategy and avoid frequent trading.

**Loss Aversion:**

The pain of losing money is psychologically more intense than the joy of gaining the same amount.

Example: Holding onto losing stocks too

long in the hope they'll recover.

**Solution:** Accept losses as part of investing and cut your losses when necessary.

**Herd Mentality:**

Following the crowd often leads to poor timing.

Example: Buying into the hype of a stock only to see its price plummet later.

Solution: Base your decisions on research rather than trends.

Strategies to Avoid Emotional Decisions

**Create an Investment Plan:**

A clear plan with defined goals, timelines, and strategies acts as a roadmap during emotional turbulence.

**Stick to the Fundamentals:**

Regularly review company financials, industry trends, and macroeconomic indicators rather than acting on news or rumors.

**Automate Investments:**

Set up automatic contributions to your

portfolio to avoid the temptation of timing the market.

**Practice Detachment:**

View your investments objectively, treating them like business decisions rather than personal achievements.

By understanding and controlling emotional triggers, you can minimize impulsive decisions and align your actions with long-term goals.

### Understanding Risk Tolerance

Risk tolerance is the level of uncertainty an investor is willing and able to endure regarding potential losses in their portfolio. Recognizing and aligning your investments with your risk tolerance is a cornerstone of successful investing.

### Factors That Determine Risk Tolerance

**Financial Situation:**

Your income, savings, and liabilities significantly influence your ability to take risks.

Example: A young professional with stable income can afford more risk compared to a retiree relying on fixed savings.

**Investment Goals:**

Short-term goals (e.g., buying a house) require low-risk investments, while long-term goals (e.g., retirement) can tolerate more volatility.

**Emotional Comfort with Loss:**

Some investors are naturally more risk-averse, while others can withstand significant market swings without stress.

**Types of Risk Tolerance**

Conservative:

Focuses on preserving capital with minimal risk.

**Investments**: Bonds, blue-chip stocks, and fixed deposits.

**Moderate:**

Balances risk and reward by mixing growth-oriented and stable investments.

**Investments:** A blend of stocks, bonds, and mutual funds.

**Aggressive:**

Seeks high returns by accepting significant volatility.

**Investments**: Small-cap stocks, emerging markets, and high-growth sectors.

### Risk vs. Reward

Understanding the risk-reward trade-off is essential. Higher returns usually require higher risk, but not all risks are worth taking.

Example: Penny stocks offer high potential returns but come with a high likelihood of failure.

### Assessing Your Risk Tolerance

**Self-Assessment Tools:**

Online questionnaires help gauge your comfort with risk.

**Consulting Financial Advisors:**

Professionals can help align your risk tolerance with your investment strategy.

By accurately assessing your risk tolerance, you can build a portfolio that suits your financial and emotional needs.

## The Importance of Patience and Discipline

Patience and discipline are often overlooked virtues in investing but are essential for long-term success. Markets are volatile, and the ability to stay the course can distinguish successful investors from those who fail.

### Why Patience Matters

**Compounding Takes Time:**

Compounding is the process of earning returns on both your original investment and previously earned returns.

Example: Warren Buffett accumulated most of his wealth after the age of 60 due to compounding.

**Market Fluctuations Are Normal:**

Short-term market movements can be unpredictable, but long-term trends usually reward patient investors.

Example: The S&P 500 has delivered average annual returns of around 8%-10% despite periodic crashes.

### Practicing Discipline

**Stick to Your Strategy:**

Avoid abandoning your investment plan due to fear or greed.

### Regularly Rebalance Your Portfolio:

Adjust your portfolio periodically to maintain your desired asset allocation.

### Avoid Overtrading:

Excessive buying and selling erode returns through fees and poor timing.

### Historical Evidence Supporting Patience

During the Great Recession (2008-2009), patient investors who stayed in the market recovered their losses and saw significant gains in the following decade.

Conversely, those who sold their investments during the downturn often missed the recovery.

### Patience as a Competitive Edge

In a world driven by instant gratification, patience gives investors a unique advantage. By focusing on long-term goals and resisting the urge to react to short-term noise, you can outperform more reactive peers.

The psychology of investing is just as important as technical and fundamental analysis. Avoiding emotional decisions, understanding your risk tolerance, and cultivating patience and discipline are critical for long-term success. By mastering these psychological aspects, you can navigate the complexities of the stock market with confidence, resilience, and clarity, ensuring your financial goals remain within reach.

# Part 2: Developing a Winning Strategy

# Chapter 4

## *Setting Clear Investment Goals*

Clear investment goals are the foundation of a successful investment strategy. Without defined objectives, your investment journey can lack direction, leading to inefficiency, missed opportunities, or financial losses. This section delves into the importance of setting well-articulated goals, defining short-term and long-term objectives, and aligning investments with your life ambitions.

### Defining Short-Term and Long-Term Objectives

### The Importance of Time Horizons

Time horizons are a crucial element of investment planning. The timeframe for achieving your financial goals influences the level of risk you can take, the types of assets you should invest in, and the expected returns.

### Short-Term Goals:

Short-term goals are those you aim to achieve within 1 to 5 years. These might include saving for a vacation, purchasing a car, or building an emergency fund. Short-term goals require low-risk investments to ensure the capital is preserved.

**Characteristics:**

Emphasis on liquidity.

Lower risk tolerance.

Predictable returns.

**Examples of Suitable Investments:**

High-yield savings accounts.

Certificates of deposit (CDs).

Treasury bills or short-term bonds.

Case Study:

Suppose you plan to buy a car in three years. Investing in volatile assets like stocks could be counterproductive because market downturns could reduce your principal when you need it. Instead, a low-risk savings product with consistent returns ensures you reach your goal.

**Long-Term Goals:**

Long-term goals are typically 10 years or more into the future and include objectives like retirement, funding children's education, or buying a home. Longer time horizons allow for more risk-taking since market volatility tends to even out over time.

**Characteristics:**

Higher risk tolerance.

Focus on growth.

Compounding plays a significant role.

**Examples of Suitable Investments:**

Stocks and equity funds.

Real estate.

Retirement accounts like 401(k)s or IRAs.

**Case Study:**

If you're saving for retirement in 20 years, a portfolio heavily weighted toward stocks can provide higher returns over the long run compared to bonds or cash equivalents.

## Steps to Define Objectives

**Identify Your Priorities:**

Make a list of financial goals, categorizing them as short-term or long-term.

**Quantify Your Goals:**

Assign a monetary value to each goal.

Example: "I need $50,000 for a down payment on a house in five years."

**Determine Deadlines:**

Specify when you want to achieve each goal.

**Assess Current Financial Standing:**

Evaluate your income, expenses, and savings to determine how much you can invest regularly.

**Calculate Required Returns:**

Use tools or consult professionals to understand the rate of return needed to achieve your goals within the specified timeframe.

By clearly defining your short-term and long-term objectives, you create a roadmap that guides your investment decisions, ensuring they are purposeful and aligned with your aspirations.

## Aligning Investments with Life Goals

Investment success is not merely about accumulating wealth; it's about achieving financial freedom and fulfilling personal ambitions. To ensure that your investments serve a purpose, you must align them with your life goals.

### Why Alignment Matters

### Clarity of Purpose:

Aligning investments with goals provides a clear sense of direction and motivation.

### Avoiding Mismanagement:

Misaligned investments can lead to overexposure to risk or missed opportunities for growth.

### Emotional Connection:

When investments are tied to meaningful goals, it's easier to stay disciplined during market fluctuations.

### Examples of Life Goals and Investment Alignment

Buying a Home:

Goal: Accumulate enough for a down payment in five years.

**Investment Strategy:** Focus on stable, low-risk assets to preserve principal.

**Retirement:**

**Goal:** Build a portfolio that provides a steady income in retirement.

Investment Strategy: Allocate funds across diversified assets, gradually reducing risk as retirement approaches.

**Children's Education:**

Goal: Save for college tuition in 15 years.

Investment Strategy: Start with equity-heavy investments and shift to safer assets as the target date nears.

**Building an Emergency Fund:**

Goal: Have six months' worth of living expenses saved.

**Investment Strategy**: Use liquid assets like money market funds or savings accounts.

**The SMART Framework for Aligning Goals**

To ensure investments are aligned with life goals, consider using the SMART framework:

Specific:

Clearly define what you want to achieve.

Example: "Save $30,000 for a wedding in three years."

Measurable:

Quantify progress to stay on track.

Example: "Save $10,000 per year for the next three years."

### Achievable:

Ensure goals are realistic given your financial situation.

Example: If you can only save $8,000 annually, adjust the goal or timeline.

### Relevant:

Align goals with your broader financial and personal priorities.

### Time-Bound:

Set clear deadlines to create a sense of urgency and discipline.

### Reviewing and Adjusting Goals

Life circumstances and financial markets are dynamic, making it essential to periodically review and adjust your investment strategy.

**Periodic Reviews:**

Evaluate your progress annually to ensure your portfolio is on track to meet your goals.

**Adjusting for Life Changes:**

Major life events like marriage, a career change, or the birth of a child may necessitate revisiting your goals.

**Rebalancing Portfolio:**

Shift allocations as your goals evolve or deadlines approach.

Setting clear investment goals and aligning them with your life aspirations are critical components of a winning investment strategy. By defining short-term and long-term objectives and ensuring your investments reflect your priorities, you create a pathway to financial success that is both purposeful and achievable. This disciplined approach not only maximizes returns but also provides the peace of mind that your money is working toward what truly matters to you.

# Chapter 5

## *Building a Strong Portfolio*

A strong portfolio is the cornerstone of successful investing. It provides a structured approach to managing your assets, maximizing returns, and mitigating risks. This chapter delves into the foundational elements of portfolio construction: the power of diversification, the principles of asset allocation, and the delicate balance between risk and reward. By understanding and implementing these principles, you can create a portfolio that aligns with your financial goals and risk tolerance.

### The Power of Diversification

Diversification is a time-tested investment strategy aimed at reducing risk by spreading investments across various assets, sectors, and geographies. The rationale is simple: don't put all your eggs in one basket.

### What Is Diversification?

Diversification involves investing in a mix of assets to reduce the impact of any single investment's poor performance on the overall portfolio. By holding a variety of assets, you can minimize risk and enhance the potential for steady returns.

**Key Benefits:**

**Risk Reduction:** Poor performance in one area may be offset by gains in another.

**Steady Returns:** A diversified portfolio tends to perform more consistently over time.

**Capital Preservation:** It helps protect your capital during market downturns.

**Types of Diversification**

**Asset Class Diversification:**

Spread investments across different asset classes like stocks, bonds, real estate, and cash equivalents.

Example: A portfolio with 50% equities, 30% bonds, and 20% real estate.

**Sector Diversification:**

Invest in various industries (e.g., technology, healthcare, energy).

Example: If the technology sector underperforms, gains in healthcare might compensate.

**Geographic Diversification:**

Allocate investments across different countries or regions to mitigate local economic risks.

Example: Combining U.S. equities with emerging markets stocks.

**Company Size Diversification:**

Invest in small-cap, mid-cap, and large-cap companies to balance growth and stability.

**Challenges of Diversification**

While diversification is beneficial, it requires careful execution.

**Over-Diversification:** Spreading investments too thin can dilute returns.

**Correlation:** Choosing assets that behave similarly during downturns defeats the purpose.

Costs: Managing a diversified portfolio can be expensive due to transaction fees and fund management costs.

Practical Example of Diversification

**Imagine a portfolio with investments in:**

Technology stocks.

Bonds.

International real estate.

Gold.

If technology stocks decline due to regulatory changes, bonds and gold may perform well, cushioning the impact on the portfolio.

### Asset Allocation Basics

Asset allocation refers to the process of dividing an investment portfolio among different asset categories, such as stocks, bonds, and cash. It is one of the most critical decisions in portfolio management, often determining the majority of a portfolio's returns.

### Why Asset Allocation Matters

Risk Management: Different assets carry varying levels of risk and return.

Goal Alignment: Proper allocation ensures your investments align with your financial objectives and risk tolerance.

Key Asset Classes

Stocks:

Represent ownership in companies.

Offer high growth potential but come with higher risk.

Best for long-term goals.

Bonds:

Fixed-income securities that provide steady returns.

Lower risk than stocks but offer less growth potential.

Suitable for income generation and risk mitigation.

**Cash and Cash Equivalents:**

Includes savings accounts, money market funds, and Treasury bills.

Low risk and high liquidity but minimal returns.

**Real Estate:**

Tangible asset class providing rental income and capital appreciation.

Acts as a hedge against inflation.

**Alternative Investments:**

Includes commodities, hedge funds, and private equity.

Can diversify a portfolio but may carry higher risk and less liquidity.

Determining the Right Asset Mix

**Age-Based Allocation:**

Younger investors can take on more risk (e.g., higher stock allocation) due to longer time horizons.

Example: "100 minus your age" rule – a 30-year-old could have 70% in stocks and 30% in bonds.

**Risk Tolerance:**

Aggressive investors might favor stocks, while conservative ones may prefer bonds and cash.

**Investment Goals:**

Retirement planning might require a balanced approach, while short-term goals favor low-risk assets.

## Rebalancing Your Portfolio

Periodic rebalancing ensures that your portfolio remains aligned with your goals.

### How to Rebalance:

Review asset allocation annually or after significant market movements.

Sell overperforming assets and reinvest in underperforming ones to maintain target allocation.

### Balancing Risk and Reward

Investing inherently involves a trade-off between risk and reward. Balancing these factors is essential to achieving a portfolio that meets your financial objectives without causing undue stress.

### Understanding Risk

Risk is the uncertainty associated with investment returns. While higher risk can lead to greater rewards, it also increases the potential for loss.

### Types of Risks:

**Market Risk**: Price fluctuations due to market conditions.

**Credit Risk:** Risk of a bond issuer defaulting.

Liquidity Risk: Difficulty in selling assets without significant price reductions.

**Inflation Risk:** The erosion of purchasing power over time.

### Risk Tolerance

**Your risk tolerance is influenced by:**

Age: Younger investors can afford more risk due to longer time horizons.

**Financial Stability:** Those with steady incomes may take on more risk.

**Personality:** Some individuals are naturally more risk-averse.

### Maximizing Rewards

**To achieve optimal returns:**

**Invest for the Long Term:** Compounding magnifies gains over time.

**Diversify:** Reduces the risk of significant losses.

**Monitor and Adjust:** Keep your portfolio aligned with your goals and market conditions.

### Balancing Techniques

### Risk-Adjusted Returns:

Evaluate investments using metrics like the Sharpe ratio to understand returns relative to risk.

### Investment Buckets:

Allocate funds into different buckets based on risk levels.

Example: A high-risk bucket for stocks, a medium-risk bucket for bonds, and a low-risk bucket for cash.

### Contingency Planning:

Set aside an emergency fund to avoid liquidating investments prematurely during financial crises.

Building a strong portfolio requires understanding the power of diversification, mastering asset allocation, and balancing risk with reward. By diversifying across asset classes, sectors, and geographies, you minimize risk while enhancing returns. Strategic asset allocation ensures your portfolio aligns with your financial goals and risk tolerance. Finally, balancing risk and reward empowers you to navigate market uncertainties with confidence, maximizing the potential of your investments. With these principles in place, you are well-equipped to create a resilient and growth-oriented portfolio.

# Chapter 6

## Stock Research and Analysis

Stock research and analysis are the backbone of informed investing. By understanding the factors that drive a company's performance and market trends, investors can make calculated decisions that align with their financial goals. This section explores three critical aspects of stock research and analysis: Fundamental Analysis, Technical Analysis, and the essential Tools and Resources for Research. Each approach complements the other and offers unique insights into the stock market.

***Fundamental Analysis:*** Reading Financial Statements

Fundamental analysis involves evaluating a company's financial health, competitive position, and future prospects by examining its financial statements and other economic factors. It focuses on understanding a company's intrinsic value, which helps investors determine whether a stock is undervalued or overvalued.

## Key Financial Statements

### Income Statement:

Shows a company's profitability over a specific period.

**Key components include:**

**Revenue:** Total income generated from sales or services.

**Cost of Goods Sold (COGS):** Direct costs associated with producing goods.

**Gross Profit:** Revenue minus COGS.

**Net Income:** The bottom line, representing profit after all expenses.

**Use in Analysis:** Assess growth trends, profit margins, and operational efficiency.

### Balance Sheet:

Provides a snapshot of a company's financial position at a specific point in time.

**Key components include:**

Assets: Resources owned by the company (e.g., cash, inventory, property).

Liabilities: Obligations owed (e.g., loans, accounts payable).

**Equity:** Owners' residual interest after liabilities are deducted from assets.

**Use in Analysis:** Evaluate liquidity, leverage, and financial stability.

### Cash Flow Statement:

Tracks the inflow and outflow of cash.

### Key sections include:

**Operating Activities:** Cash generated from core business operations.

**Investing Activities:** Cash spent on or generated from investments.

**Financing Activities**: Cash from debt, equity, or dividend payments.

**Use in Analysis**: Assess the company's ability to generate cash and sustain operations.

### Key Ratios in Fundamental Analysis

### Profitability Ratios:

**Net Profit Margin:** Measures profit as a percentage of revenue.

Return on Equity (ROE): Indicates how efficiently equity is used to generate profits.

**Liquidity Ratios:**

**Current Ratio**: Current assets divided by current liabilities, indicating short-term financial health.

**Valuation Ratios:**

**Price-to-Earnings (P/E) Ratio:** Compares stock price to earnings per share, reflecting market expectations.

**Price-to-Book (P/B) Ratio:** Compares stock price to book value per share, highlighting intrinsic worth.

**Qualitative Factors**

Fundamental analysis isn't just about numbers. Consider qualitative factors such as:

**Management Quality:** Leadership's experience and track record.

**Competitive Advantage**: Unique strengths that differentiate the company.

**Industry Trends:** Broader trends that influence the sector.

**Technical Analysis**: Understanding Charts and Indicators

Technical analysis involves studying price movements and trading volumes to predict future price trends. It is based on the assumption that all market factors are already reflected in stock prices and that patterns tend to repeat over time.

## Core Principles of Technical Analysis

Market Action Discounts Everything: Stock prices reflect all relevant information.

**Prices Move in Trends**: Recognizing uptrends, downtrends, and sideways trends is crucial.

**History Tends to Repeat Itself:** Patterns in the market often recur.

## Key Tools in Technical Analysis

**Charts:**

Line Chart: Simplest form, connecting closing prices over time.

**Bar Chart:** Shows opening, closing, high, and low prices.

**Candlestick Chart:** Highlights price movements with color-coded bars.

**Indicators:**

**Moving Averages (MA):** Smooth out price data to identify trends.

Example: 50-day MA vs. 200-day MA to determine short- and long-term trends.

**Relative Strength Index (RSI):** Measures momentum and identifies overbought or oversold conditions.

Range: 0-100, with levels above 70 indicating overbought and below 30 indicating oversold.

**Bollinger Bands:** Show volatility by creating upper and lower bands around a moving average.

**MACD (Moving Average Convergence Divergence):** Indicates changes in momentum by comparing two moving averages.

### Patterns in Technical Analysis

**Trend Patterns:**

**Head and Shoulders:** Predicts a reversal of an uptrend.

**Double Top/Bottom:** Indicates a reversal in price direction.

**Continuation Patterns:**

**Flags and Pennants:** Suggest a brief consolidation before the trend resumes.

**Triangles:** Show tightening price ranges that break out in the direction of the trend.

### Volume Analysis

Increased trading volume often confirms the validity of a price movement.

Example: A breakout from a resistance level accompanied by high volume is more reliable.

### Tools and Resources for Research

Effective stock research relies on access to the right tools and resources. These tools provide data, insights, and analytics essential for making informed decisions.

### Financial News Platforms

**Bloomberg:** Comprehensive global market data and news.

**Reuters:** Reliable financial reporting and economic news.

**CNBC:** Live updates and expert analysis on financial markets.

### Stock Screeners

**Finviz:** Filters stocks based on criteria like P/E ratio, dividend yield, and sector.

**Yahoo Finance:** Offers customizable screeners and in-depth analytics.

**Morningstar:** Provides ratings, research, and screening tools.

### Trading Platforms

**Robinhood:** User-friendly platform for beginners.

**E*TRADE:** Advanced tools for experienced traders.

**Interactive Brokers:** Low-cost platform with robust research tools.

### Research Reports

**Analyst Reports:** Detailed company analysis with buy/sell recommendations.

**Earnings Transcripts:** Insights into a company's performance and management outlook.

### Educational Resources

**Books:**

The Intelligent Investor by Benjamin Graham.

Technical Analysis of the Financial Markets by John J. Murphy.

**Online Courses:** Platforms like Coursera and Udemy offer courses on stock market investing.

**Social Media and Forums**

**Twitter:** Follow analysts and financial experts.

Reddit: Subreddits like r/investing for community-driven insights.

Stock research and analysis are essential for navigating the complexities of the stock market. By mastering fundamental analysis, investors can evaluate a company's financial health and intrinsic value. Technical analysis complements this by providing insights into market trends and price movements. Armed with the right tools and resources, investors can make informed decisions, reducing risk and maximizing returns. Whether you are a beginner or an experienced investor, these principles will serve as the foundation for achieving your financial goals.

# Chapter 7

## *Timing the Market vs. Time in the Market*

The debate between timing the market and time in the market is one of the most discussed topics in investing. While the allure of timing the market to buy low and sell high is tempting, the data overwhelmingly supports the value of staying invested over the long term. This chapter explores these two strategies, debunks the myths surrounding market timing, and emphasizes the benefits of adopting a long-term investment perspective.

## *Debunking Market Timing Myths*

Market timing involves predicting future price movements to buy at the lowest point and sell at the highest. While this idea may seem logical in theory, it is nearly impossible to execute consistently in practice. Here's why market timing is riddled with challenges and misconceptions:

### 1. Predicting the Market Is Almost Impossible

**Volatility and Uncertainty:** The stock market

is influenced by countless factors, including geopolitical events, economic indicators, and investor sentiment. Predicting these variables with accuracy is unrealistic.

**Historical Evidence:** Studies show that even professional investors struggle to time the market successfully. For example, a study by DALBAR revealed that individual investors consistently underperform the market due to poor timing decisions.

### 2. The Cost of Missing the Best Days

Missing just a few of the market's best-performing days can significantly reduce returns.

Example: According to J.P. Morgan, from 2000 to 2020, if an investor missed the 10 best days in the S&P 500, their annualized return dropped from 6.06% to 2.44%.

The best days often occur during periods of high volatility, which are the times most investors tend to stay out of the market.

### 3. Emotional Decision-Making

Market timing often leads to fear-based selling during downturns and greedy buying during upturns, which results in buying high and selling low.

Behavioral finance studies highlight how emotions like fear and greed impair rational decision-making.

### 4. Costs and Taxes

Transaction Costs: Frequent buying and selling increase trading fees, reducing overall returns.

**Tax Implications:** Short-term gains are often taxed at a higher rate than long-term capital gains, further eroding profits.

### The Value of a Long-Term Perspective

Instead of trying to time the market, focusing on time in the market has consistently proven to be a more reliable strategy for wealth building. This approach involves staying invested for extended periods, allowing the power of compounding and market recovery to work in your favor.

### 1. The Power of Compounding

Definition: Compounding occurs when your investments generate earnings, and those earnings, in turn, generate additional earnings.

Example: A $10,000 investment with a 7% annual return grows to $76,122 in 30 years, even without additional contributions.

Key Insight: The longer you remain invested, the more compounding amplifies your returns.

### 2. Market Recovery Over Time

Historical data shows that markets recover from downturns and continue to grow in the long term.

Example: After the 2008 financial crisis, the S&P 500 dropped nearly 40% but recovered fully within a few years, delivering strong returns for those who stayed invested.

By remaining patient, investors can benefit from market rebounds rather than locking in losses by selling during downturns.

### 3. Consistency Beats Perfection

Dollar-Cost Averaging (DCA): Investing a fixed amount regularly, regardless of market conditions, reduces the risk of buying at market peaks.

Example: If you invest $500 monthly, you buy more shares when prices are low and fewer shares when prices are high, averaging out your cost over time.

Staying consistent ensures that you benefit from market growth without the stress of trying to time your entries and exits.

### 4. Historical Performance of Major Indexes

Over the past century, major indexes like the S&P 500 have delivered average annual returns of 7-10%.

Despite short-term volatility, the long-term upward trajectory of the market rewards patient investors.

Key Differences Between Timing the Market and Time in the Market

Aspect Timing the Market      Time in the Market

Approach     Active, speculative attempts to predict highs and lows.     Passive, focused on staying invested long-term.

Risk Level     High, due to unpredictability and frequent trading.     Lower, as it minimizes emotional decisions.

Returns     Inconsistent and often underperform market averages.     Consistent, benefiting from compounding and recovery.

Emotional Impact    Stressful, requires constant monitoring and decisions.    Calmer, requires discipline and patience.

Cost Implications    Higher, due to trading fees and short-term taxes.    Lower, due to minimal trading activity.

**Real-Life Examples and Case Studies**

Example 1: The 2008 Financial Crisis

Many investors exited the market out of fear during the 2008 crash.

Those who stayed invested saw their portfolios recover and grow significantly as the market rebounded in the following years.

Example 2: Warren Buffett's Philosophy

Buffett famously avoids market timing, emphasizing the importance of holding quality stocks for the long term.

His long-term investments in companies like Coca-Cola and Apple highlight the success of patience over speculation.

Example 3: The COVID-19 Market Crash

In March 2020, global markets plummeted

due to the pandemic.

Investors who sold during the panic missed the rapid recovery that followed, with the S&P 500 reaching all-time highs within months.

**Practical Tips for Staying Invested Long-Term**

**Define Your Investment Goals:**

Establish clear short-term and long-term objectives to stay focused during market fluctuations.

**Adopt a Diversified Portfolio:**

Spread your investments across asset classes, sectors, and geographies to reduce risk.

**Ignore Noise:**

Avoid reacting to daily market news and focus on the bigger picture.

**Automate Your Investments:**

Use tools like automatic contributions to ensure consistent investing without emotional interference.

**Rebalance Periodically:**

Adjust your portfolio to maintain your desired asset allocation as markets move.

**Stay Educated:**

Continuously learn about the markets and your investments to build confidence and reduce fear.

The choice between timing the market and time in the market is pivotal for investors seeking long-term success. While the appeal of market timing may be strong, the evidence strongly supports the superiority of staying invested for the long haul. By understanding the risks and limitations of market timing, adopting a long-term perspective, and leveraging strategies like diversification and dollar-cost averaging, investors can build wealth more consistently and effectively. Time, patience, and discipline remain the most powerful allies in the journey to financial freedom.

# Part 3: Practical Investing Techniques

## Chapter 8

### Getting Started with Your First Investment

Investing in the stock market can seem intimidating, especially for beginners. However, understanding the foundational steps—choosing a brokerage platform, learning how to place your first trade, and selecting the right investment options—can demystify the process and set you on the path to financial growth. This section provides a detailed, step-by-step guide to getting started and explains key investment options like index funds and exchange-traded funds (ETFs).

### Choosing a Brokerage Platform

The first step in your investment journey is selecting a brokerage platform. This is the intermediary through which you will buy and sell stocks, ETFs, mutual funds, and other securities.

#### 1. Types of Brokerage Accounts

**Full-Service Brokers:**

Offer personalized advice, portfolio management, and a wide range of services.

Ideal for individuals who prefer a hands-on approach or need expert guidance.

Example: Merrill Lynch, Morgan Stanley.

Drawback: Higher fees compared to other options.

**Discount Brokers:**

Provide basic trading platforms with lower fees.

Suitable for self-directed investors who prefer to make their own decisions.

Examples: Charles Schwab, Fidelity, TD Ameritrade.

**Robo-Advisors:**

Automated platforms that use algorithms to manage your portfolio.

Best for passive investors who want a hands-off approach.

Examples: Betterment, Wealthfront.

**2. Key Features to Consider**

**Fees and Commissions:**

Look for platforms offering zero-commission trades or low fees.

Be aware of hidden fees, such as account maintenance charges.

**Ease of Use:**

User-friendly interfaces make it easier for beginners to navigate.

Mobile app availability is an added advantage for on-the-go access.

**Research Tools and Education:**

Platforms offering educational resources, stock screeners, and financial analysis tools are invaluable for new investors.

**Account Types:**

Options include taxable accounts, traditional IRAs, and Roth IRAs.

Choose based on your investment goals and tax strategy.

### 3. Steps to Open an Account

Gather personal identification and financial details, such as your Social Security Number

(SSN), employment information, and bank account details.

Complete the online or in-person application.

Fund your account through a bank transfer, check deposit, or wire transfer.

## How to Place Your First Trade

Once your brokerage account is set up, the next step is to place your first trade. This may seem daunting, but it's a straightforward process with a little preparation.

### 1. Understand the Types of Orders

**Market Order:**

Buys or sells a stock at the current market price.

Best for stocks with high liquidity and minimal price fluctuations.

**Limit Order:**

Sets a specific price at which you are willing to buy or sell.

Provides more control but may not execute if the market price doesn't meet your limit.

**Stop-Loss Order:**

Sells a stock automatically if it falls to a certain price, protecting against large losses.

**Stop-Limit Order:**

Combines the features of stop-loss and limit orders, giving you more control over execution.

### 2. Research Before Trading

Use the brokerage platform's research tools to analyze potential investments.

Review key metrics such as price-to-earnings (P/E) ratio, dividend yield, and recent price trends.

### 3. Steps to Execute a Trade

Log into your brokerage account and navigate to the trading section.

Select the stock or ETF you want to buy.

Enter the ticker symbol (e.g., AAPL for Apple, AMZN for Amazon).

Choose the type of order (market, limit, etc.).

Specify the number of shares or dollar amount to invest.

Review and confirm the transaction.

### 4. Monitor Your Investment

After making your first trade, track its performance using your brokerage platform.

Avoid overreacting to short-term fluctuations, especially if you're investing for the long term.

### Index Funds and ETFs

For beginners and seasoned investors alike, index funds and ETFs are among the most popular investment options. They provide diversification, simplicity, and low costs, making them an excellent choice for building a robust portfolio.

### Why Passive Investing Works

### 1. Consistent Returns

Index funds and ETFs track the performance of a specific market index, such as the S&P 500 or the Nasdaq 100.

Over the long term, these funds often outperform actively managed funds due to their lower fees and consistent market exposure.

## 2. Reduced Costs

Passive funds have lower expense ratios compared to actively managed funds.

Example: Vanguard's S&P 500 ETF (VOO) has an expense ratio of just 0.03%.

Lower costs mean more of your money remains invested and compounding over time.

## 3. Simplicity and Transparency

With passive funds, you know exactly what you're investing in.

Example: An S&P 500 index fund holds shares in the 500 largest U.S. companies.

This transparency simplifies investment decisions for beginners.

## How to Pick the Right Funds

### 1. Define Your Investment Goals

Are you saving for retirement, building wealth, or achieving specific short-term goals?

Your goals will determine whether you focus on growth-oriented funds, income-generating funds, or a balanced mix.

## 2. Evaluate Key Metrics

Expense Ratio: The annual fee charged by the fund. Lower is better.

**Tracking Error:** Measures how closely the fund follows its benchmark index. Lower tracking errors indicate better performance.

Liquidity: Highly liquid funds allow for easy buying and selling without affecting the price.

## 3. Diversify Across Sectors and Regions

Choose funds covering different sectors (technology, healthcare, finance) and regions (U.S., Europe, emerging markets).

Diversification reduces risk by spreading investments across multiple industries and geographies.

## 4. Consider Dividend ETFs

For investors seeking income, dividend-focused ETFs can provide regular payouts.

Example: Vanguard Dividend Appreciation ETF (VIG).

## 5. Assess Performance Over Time

Avoid funds with high short-term gains but

poor long-term performance. Look for consistent returns over 5, 10, or 15 years.

### Real-Life Examples of Index Funds and ETFs

**1. Vanguard Total Stock Market Index Fund (VTSAX)**

Tracks the performance of the entire U.S. stock market, providing comprehensive diversification.

Ideal for long-term investors seeking broad exposure.

**2. SPDR S&P 500 ETF (SPY)**

The first ETF ever created, SPY tracks the S&P 500.

A popular choice for investors seeking exposure to large-cap U.S. companies.

**3. iShares MSCI Emerging Markets ETF (EEM)**

Focuses on stocks from emerging economies like China, India, and Brazil.

Suitable for investors looking to diversify internationally.

Getting started with your first investment is

a transformative step toward financial independence. By choosing the right brokerage platform, understanding how to execute trades, and focusing on passive investment vehicles like index funds and ETFs, you can build a portfolio that aligns with your goals and withstands market volatility. The journey may seem daunting initially, but with knowledge, discipline, and a long-term perspective, you can set yourself up for success in the stock market.

# Chapter 9

## *Dividend Investing for Steady Income*

Dividend investing is a strategy that focuses on purchasing stocks from companies that regularly distribute a portion of their earnings to shareholders in the form of dividends. This approach provides investors with a steady income stream, making it especially appealing to retirees, income-focused investors, and those looking to build long-term wealth through reinvestment. In this section, we will explore the nuances of dividend investing, the differences between high-yield and dividend growth stocks, and the benefits of reinvesting dividends for compounding returns.

## *Understanding Dividend Investing*

Dividend investing revolves around selecting stocks that provide regular payouts to investors. These payments typically occur quarterly but can vary depending on the company. Here's why dividends are a crucial aspect of a successful investment portfolio:

### 1. Predictable Income Stream

Dividends act as a consistent source of income, regardless of stock price fluctuations.

For retirees or those seeking passive income, this predictability is a significant advantage.

## 2. Indication of Financial Health

Companies that consistently pay dividends are often financially stable with robust cash flows.

A growing dividend payout signals confidence in future earnings.

## 3. Lower Volatility

Dividend-paying stocks tend to be less volatile than growth stocks, offering a level of stability during market downturns.

## High-Yield vs. Dividend Growth Stocks

Investors often debate between focusing on high-yield stocks or dividend growth stocks. Both have their merits, but understanding their characteristics is key to aligning them with your financial goals.

## High-Yield Stocks

High-yield stocks are those with a high dividend yield, calculated as the annual dividend divided by the stock's current price.

## Advantages:

### Immediate Income:

High-yield stocks generate significant income quickly, making them ideal for retirees or investors needing cash flow.

### Attractive for Income Seekers:

A higher yield means a greater return on investment through dividends.

## Risks:

### Potential for Dividend Cuts:

A high yield may indicate financial distress if the payout is unsustainable.

Example: A company struggling to maintain profitability may cut its dividend to preserve cash.

### Limited Growth Potential:

High-yield stocks are often mature companies with slower earnings growth.

They may lack the capital to reinvest in expansion, limiting stock price appreciation.

## Examples of High-Yield Stocks:

Utility companies (e.g., Duke Energy, Southern Company).

Real Estate Investment Trusts (REITs), such as Realty Income Corporation.

### Dividend Growth Stocks

Dividend growth stocks focus on companies that regularly increase their dividend payments.

**Advantages:**

**Compounding Returns:**

Consistently rising dividends can lead to exponential income growth over time.

Example: A 5% annual dividend increase doubles your income in approximately 14 years.

**Strong Financial Fundamentals:**

Companies with a history of dividend growth are often well-managed and financially sound.

**Stock Price Appreciation:**

Dividend growth often correlates with increasing earnings and stock price appreciation, offering a dual benefit.

Risks:

**Lower Initial Yield:**

Dividend growth stocks typically offer a lower starting yield compared to high-yield stocks.

This requires patience to reap the long-term benefits.

**Market Sensitivity:**

Dividend growth stocks can be more sensitive to market changes, particularly interest rate fluctuations.

**Examples of Dividend Growth Stocks:**

Procter & Gamble, Johnson & Johnson, and Microsoft.

Choosing Between High-Yield and Dividend Growth Stocks

**The choice depends on your financial objectives:**

Income Now: High-yield stocks are better suited for those needing immediate cash flow.

Income Later: Dividend growth stocks are ideal for long-term wealth accumulation.

A balanced portfolio often includes a mix of both to optimize income and growth potential.

Reinvesting Dividends for Compounding Returns

One of the most powerful aspects of dividend investing is the ability to reinvest dividends. This strategy allows you to purchase additional shares of the stock, leading to exponential growth in both your income and capital over time.

## How Dividend Reinvestment Works

### Dividends Are Paid:

Companies distribute dividends to shareholders.

### Dividends Are Reinvested:

Instead of receiving cash, dividends are used to buy more shares of the same stock.

### Growth Through Compounding:

Each reinvested dividend earns its own dividends in future periods, creating a compounding effect.

## Benefits of Reinvesting Dividends

### Accelerated Portfolio Growth:

Reinvesting allows you to accumulate more shares without additional capital investment.

Example: A $10,000 investment with a 4% yield and 5% dividend growth annually grows to $27,000 in 20 years if dividends are reinvested.

### Dollar-Cost Averaging:

Reinvesting dividends ensures that you purchase more shares when prices are low and fewer shares when prices are high, reducing the impact of market volatility.

### Tax Advantages in Retirement Accounts:

In tax-advantaged accounts like IRAs or 401(k)s, reinvesting dividends incurs no immediate tax liability, allowing your portfolio to grow tax-free.

### Dividend Reinvestment Plans (DRIPs)

Most companies and brokerages offer Dividend Reinvestment Plans (DRIPs), which automate the reinvestment process.

### Advantages of DRIPs:

No additional fees for reinvestment.

Fractional shares can be purchased, maximizing every dollar.

Disciplined investment approach without emotional decision-making.

**Considerations:**

In taxable accounts, reinvested dividends are still subject to taxes, so keep track of your cost basis.

Real-Life Example of Compounding Through Reinvestment

**Consider an investment in Johnson & Johnson:**

Initial Investment: $10,000.

Dividend Yield: 2.5%.

Annual Dividend Growth Rate: 6%.

Stock Price Appreciation: 4% annually.

**If dividends are reinvested:**

After 10 years, your portfolio grows to approximately $17,000.

After 20 years, it doubles to $34,000.

The power of reinvesting dividends combined with compounding returns amplifies wealth creation over time.

## Strategies for Dividend Investors

**Start Early:**

The earlier you invest, the more time compounding has to work.

**Diversify Your Dividend Portfolio:**

Spread investments across industries and regions to minimize risk.

**Monitor Dividend Sustainability:**

Pay attention to payout ratios and earnings trends to ensure dividends are sustainable.

**Focus on Total Return:**

While dividends are essential, consider capital appreciation as part of your overall strategy.

Dividend investing is a proven strategy for generating steady income and building long-term wealth. Whether you prioritize high-yield stocks for immediate income or dividend growth stocks for compounding returns, aligning your investment choices with your financial goals is critical. By reinvesting dividends, you can leverage the power of compounding to maximize your portfolio's growth. With a disciplined approach and careful stock selection, dividend investing can be a cornerstone of a successful investment strategy.

# Chapter 10

## *Growth Investing Strategies*

Growth investing is a dynamic and rewarding approach that focuses on identifying companies with the potential for substantial earnings growth over time. This strategy emphasizes capital appreciation over dividends or short-term gains, making it an attractive option for investors looking to maximize long-term returns. In this section, we will explore the strategies for identifying high-potential companies and assessing the risks associated with growth stocks.

## *What is Growth Investing?*

Growth investing involves purchasing shares in companies that are expected to grow at an above-average rate compared to their peers or the overall market. These companies reinvest their earnings to fuel further expansion, often at the expense of paying dividends. While growth investing can yield high returns, it requires thorough research and a willingness to accept higher risks.

**Identifying High-Potential Companies**

The cornerstone of growth investing lies in spotting companies with significant growth potential. Here's how to identify such opportunities:

## 1. Look for Companies in Expanding Industries

High-growth companies often operate in industries experiencing rapid expansion or technological innovation. These sectors create opportunities for businesses to capture new markets and grow revenue.

Examples:

**Technology:** Cloud computing, artificial intelligence, and renewable energy.

**Healthcare:** Biotechnology and telemedicine.

Consumer Goods: E-commerce and direct-to-consumer brands.

**Key Considerations:**

Is the industry poised for long-term growth?

Does the company have a competitive advantage or unique value proposition?

## 2. Analyze Revenue Growth

A hallmark of high-potential companies is

consistent and substantial revenue growth. Growth investors look for businesses that demonstrate year-over-year increases in sales, often exceeding the industry average.

**Metrics to Monitor:**

**Revenue Growth Rate:** Companies with annual revenue growth exceeding 15-20% are considered high growth.

**Quarterly Growth Trends:** Steady growth across multiple quarters suggests stability and execution capability.

### 3. Evaluate the Business Model

A scalable and efficient business model is crucial for sustained growth. Companies with scalable operations can expand without proportionally increasing costs, leading to improved profit margins.

**Questions to Ask:**

Does the company have a scalable business model?

Is the revenue recurring (e.g., subscription-based services)?

Are there high barriers to entry protecting the business from competition?

## 4. Consider the Management Team

The leadership team plays a pivotal role in driving a company's growth. Experienced and visionary executives can navigate challenges and capitalize on opportunities.

**What to Look For:**

A proven track record of success.

Transparent communication with shareholders.

Alignment of management goals with investor interests (e.g., ownership stakes).

## 5. Examine Market Share and Competitive Position

Companies with a dominant market share or innovative products often outpace competitors. These businesses can leverage their position to enter new markets or expand their customer base.

**Key Questions:**

Does the company lead its industry?

What sets its products or services apart?

Can it sustain or grow its market share over time?

## 6. Focus on Innovation and R&D

High-growth companies prioritize research and development (R&D) to create innovative products or improve existing ones. This innovation often translates into a competitive edge and future growth potential.

**Indicators of Innovation:**

Significant investment in R&D (measured as a percentage of revenue).

Patents or intellectual property.

A pipeline of new products or services.

## 7. Assess Financial Health

While growth companies often reinvest earnings, maintaining financial stability is essential. A solid balance sheet allows companies to weather economic downturns and continue expanding.

**Metrics to Review:**

Debt-to-Equity Ratio: A low ratio suggests manageable debt levels.

Free Cash Flow (FCF): Positive FCF indicates the company generates sufficient cash to fund operations and growth.

**Profit Margins:** While growth companies may have lower margins initially, improving margins over time signal operational efficiency.

### Assessing Risk in Growth Stocks

Growth investing inherently involves higher risk due to the speculative nature of future earnings. However, understanding and mitigating these risks is crucial for long-term success.

### 1. Market Volatility

Growth stocks are highly sensitive to market conditions and macroeconomic factors. They tend to experience more significant price fluctuations than value or dividend stocks.

**How to Mitigate:**

Diversify your portfolio across sectors and industries.

Avoid overexposure to a single stock or sector.

Invest for the long term to ride out short-term volatility.

## 2. Valuation Risks

Growth stocks often trade at premium valuations, such as high price-to-earnings (P/E) or price-to-sales (P/S) ratios. While this reflects investor optimism, overpaying for a stock can lead to losses if the company fails to meet growth expectations.

**Key Valuation Metrics:**

Compare the P/E and P/S ratios to industry averages.

Use the PEG (Price/Earnings to Growth) ratio to account for growth rates.

Analyze forward-looking metrics to assess whether the premium is justified.

## 3. Earnings Volatility

Many growth companies, especially startups, have inconsistent or negative earnings. While reinvestment is necessary for growth, it increases the risk of financial instability.

**How to Evaluate:**

Examine cash flow and liquidity.

Assess whether revenue growth aligns with

increased operating expenses.

## 4. Competitive Pressure

High-growth industries attract intense competition, which can erode market share and profit margins. Companies must continuously innovate to maintain their competitive edge.

**How to Assess:**

Identify the company's competitive moat (e.g., brand loyalty, technology, or economies of scale).

Monitor competitor activities and market trends.

## 5. Regulatory and Political Risks

Growth sectors like technology and healthcare are subject to changing regulations and political scrutiny. Adverse policies or legal challenges can impact a company's growth trajectory.

**Mitigation Strategies:**

Stay informed about regulatory changes affecting the industry.

Diversify investments globally to reduce

exposure to country-specific risks.

## 6. Economic Cycles

Growth stocks are often more vulnerable to economic downturns. During periods of economic uncertainty, investors may shift to safer assets, causing growth stocks to underperform.

**How to Prepare:**

Maintain a portion of your portfolio in defensive sectors or dividend-paying stocks.

Build an emergency fund to avoid liquidating growth investments during market downturns.

**Balancing Growth and Risk**

While growth investing offers significant upside potential, maintaining a balanced approach is essential:

**Risk Tolerance:**

Assess your financial goals, time horizon, and ability to withstand losses before investing in growth stocks.

**Diversification:**

Include a mix of growth, value, and dividend-paying stocks in your portfolio.

**Research:**

Conduct thorough due diligence on each stock, focusing on fundamentals and growth prospects.

**Patience:**

Growth investing requires a long-term mindset to allow compounding and market dynamics to work in your favor.

Growth investing is a powerful strategy for building wealth, but it requires careful research and risk management. By focusing on high-potential companies, understanding their competitive advantages, and assessing risks effectively, investors can position themselves to achieve substantial long-term returns. Balancing the excitement of high growth with disciplined analysis ensures that growth investing remains a rewarding journey.

# Chapter 11

## *Value Investing*

Value investing is a disciplined investment strategy that focuses on identifying and purchasing stocks trading below their intrinsic value. This approach, popularized by legendary investors such as Benjamin Graham and Warren Buffett, emphasizes patience, deep analysis, and a commitment to long-term growth. Unlike growth investing, value investing is rooted in the principle of seeking bargains in the stock market and taking advantage of market inefficiencies.

## *What is Value Investing?*

Value investing involves buying stocks that appear undervalued based on their financial performance and future prospects. These stocks are often overlooked or undervalued due to market sentiment, short-term challenges, or external factors, but they hold the potential for significant appreciation when the market eventually recognizes their true worth.

### Finding Undervalued Stocks

To excel in value investing, investors must develop the skill of identifying stocks that are trading below their intrinsic value. Here are the key steps and considerations:

## 1. Understanding Intrinsic Value

The concept of intrinsic value refers to the true worth of a stock, determined by its fundamentals rather than its current market price. Calculating intrinsic value requires an analysis of a company's financial statements, growth potential, and market position.

**Approaches to Estimating Intrinsic Value:**

Discounted Cash Flow (DCF) Analysis: Projects future cash flows and discounts them to present value.

Book Value Analysis: Focuses on the company's assets and liabilities.

Comparable Analysis: Compares the company's valuation metrics to industry peers.

## 2. Key Financial Ratios to Identify Undervalued Stocks

Financial ratios are essential tools for assessing a stock's value. Below are some commonly used metrics:

**Price-to-Earnings (P/E) Ratio:**

Compares a company's stock price to its earnings per share (EPS). A lower P/E ratio often indicates an undervalued stock.

Example: A company with a P/E of 10 may be undervalued compared to an industry average of 15.

**Price-to-Book (P/B) Ratio:**

Compares a stock's price to its book value (assets minus liabilities). A P/B ratio below 1 often signals undervaluation.

**Dividend Yield:**

Measures the annual dividend as a percentage of the stock's price. A high dividend yield can indicate undervaluation if the company maintains strong fundamentals.

**Debt-to-Equity Ratio:**

Assesses the company's leverage. A lower ratio indicates financial stability, making the stock a potentially safer investment.

**3. Assessing the Margin of Safety**

The "margin of safety" is a core concept in

value investing. It represents the difference between a stock's intrinsic value and its market price. Investors aim to buy stocks with a substantial margin of safety to reduce downside risk.

**How to Calculate:**

Estimate the intrinsic value using financial models.

Compare it to the current market price.

Invest only when the price is significantly lower than the estimated value.

**4. Analyzing Market Sentiment**

Market sentiment often creates opportunities for value investors. Stocks may become undervalued due to:

Negative news or temporary setbacks.

Broader market corrections or sell-offs.

Misunderstood earnings reports or management changes.

Example: A well-managed company might experience a short-term price decline due to temporary issues, creating a buying opportunity for value investors.

## 5. Focusing on Quality Companies

Value investing isn't just about finding cheap stocks—it's about identifying quality businesses that are undervalued.

**Characteristics of Quality Companies:**

Strong competitive advantage (economic moat).

Consistent earnings and revenue growth.

High return on equity (ROE) and return on assets (ROA).

Resilient business models with the ability to adapt to market changes.

## The Legacy of Benjamin Graham and Warren Buffett

Benjamin Graham and Warren Buffett are synonymous with value investing. Their principles and practices have shaped the way countless investors approach the market.

**Benjamin Graham:** The Father of Value Investing

Benjamin Graham laid the foundation for value investing with his groundbreaking works, including "The Intelligent Investor" and "Security Analysis." His methods emphasized the importance of a disciplined, analytical approach to investing.

**Key Contributions:**

Margin of Safety: Investing only when the stock's price is significantly below its intrinsic value.

**Mr. Market:** Viewing the stock market as a moody partner whose offers should be evaluated rationally.

**Focus on Fundamentals:** Using financial ratios and intrinsic value calculations to assess investments.

Example: Graham's investment in undervalued stocks during the Great Depression showcased the power of value investing, as many of these stocks recovered and yielded significant returns.

**Warren Buffett:** The Modern Icon of Value Investing

Warren Buffett, a protégé of Benjamin Graham, has taken value investing to new heights. Through his company, Berkshire Hathaway, Buffett has consistently delivered exceptional returns by applying value investing principles with a focus on long-term ownership of high-quality businesses.

**Key Principles of Buffett's Strategy:**

**Invest in Businesses You Understand:** Focus on industries and companies within your circle of competence.

**Seek Durable Competitive Advantages:** Invest in companies with strong brands, cost advantages, or unique products.

**Buy and Hold:** Buffett advocates for long-term ownership, allowing investments to compound over time.

**Focus on Management Quality:** Invest in companies led by competent and ethical management teams.

**Ignore Market Noise:** Avoid short-term market distractions and focus on the underlying value of your investments.

Example: Buffett's investment in Coca-Cola in the late 1980s highlights his strategy of buying high-quality companies at reasonable prices and holding them for decades.

## The Role of Patience and Discipline in Value Investing

Value investing is not about quick wins; it's about cultivating patience and maintaining discipline. Investors must be willing to:

Wait for the right opportunities.

Hold investments during market volatility.

Stick to their analysis, even when the market disagrees.

## Risks of Value Investing

While value investing is a proven strategy, it is not without risks:

**Value Traps:** Stocks that appear undervalued but lack growth potential due to fundamental weaknesses.

**Prolonged Market Mispricing:** The market may take years to recognize a stock's intrinsic value.

**Economic and Industry Changes:** Structural shifts can erode the value of businesses in certain sectors.

Value investing remains one of the most reliable and rewarding strategies for building long-term wealth. By focusing on undervalued stocks, adhering to principles established by Benjamin Graham and Warren Buffett, and maintaining patience and discipline, investors can navigate market uncertainties and achieve consistent returns. While it requires diligence, research, and emotional fortitude, the rewards of value investing are unparalleled for those willing to stay the course.

# Part 4: Managing and Growing Your Investments

## Chapter 12

Investing is not a one-time event but a continuous process. A crucial aspect of successful investing is actively managing and growing your portfolio over time. Whether you're a novice investor or an experienced one, the ability to monitor your portfolio and adjust your strategy as circumstances change is vital for long-term success. In this section, we will explore how to monitor and adjust your investments, the key decision-making processes regarding when to buy, hold, or sell, and the importance of rebalancing strategies.

### *Monitoring and Adjusting Your Portfolio*

To maintain a successful investment strategy, it's essential to monitor your portfolio regularly and make adjustments when necessary. This process involves evaluating the performance of your investments, understanding how they align with your long-term goals, and determining whether any changes are needed to improve the portfolio's performance or better align with your risk tolerance. Here's a detailed look at how to monitor and adjust your portfolio:

## 1. Regularly Review Your Portfolio's Performance

Monitoring your portfolio is more than just checking your account balance occasionally. It's about understanding the current and projected performance of your investments in relation to your financial goals. A detailed review includes:

Performance Comparison: Track how each asset or investment in your portfolio is performing. Compare them to appropriate benchmarks, like the S&P 500 for U.S. stocks or relevant industry indexes for sector-specific investments.

**Returns on Investment (ROI):** Calculate both short-term and long-term returns to assess whether your investments are meeting your expectations. This analysis should include dividends, capital gains, and any realized or unrealized profits or losses.

**Risk Assessment:** Assess whether your portfolio is appropriately diversified and whether the risk level is in line with your current risk tolerance. You may need to adjust your risk exposure if your goals have shifted or if you are nearing a financial milestone like retirement.

## 2. Track Economic and Market Trends

While monitoring your portfolio's performance is vital, it's equally essential to stay updated on economic and market conditions that could impact your investments. By tracking broader market trends, you can adjust your portfolio accordingly. For example:

**Interest Rates and Inflation:** Rising interest rates often impact the performance of stocks, particularly those in interest-sensitive sectors like utilities or real estate. Inflation can erode the purchasing power of your returns, so monitoring inflation trends is crucial for long-term planning.

**Industry and Sector Movements:** Some sectors or industries perform better during specific economic cycles. For instance, consumer discretionary stocks might perform well during periods of economic expansion, while utilities and healthcare stocks could outperform in recessionary periods. Understanding sector rotations can help you identify when to adjust your portfolio.

**Global Events and Geopolitical Risks:** Natural disasters, political instability, and global trade tensions can have significant effects on global markets. By being aware of these events, you can make informed decisions to minimize risks or take advantage of potential opportunities.

### 3. Align Your Portfolio with Changing Financial Goals

Over time, your financial goals may evolve due to changes in your personal life, career, or retirement plans. Regularly reassess your investment strategy to ensure it aligns with your current goals and adjust your portfolio accordingly. For example:

**Goal-Based Adjustments:** If you're approaching retirement, you might want to shift from a growth-focused portfolio to one that prioritizes income and stability, such as dividend-paying stocks, bonds, or other low-risk investments.

**Life Changes:** Major life events, such as marriage, the birth of a child, or buying a home, may require you to revise your financial goals and investment strategy. Similarly, changes in your career, such as a promotion or job change, might provide new opportunities for saving and investing.

**Income Needs:** Your portfolio may need adjustments if your income needs change, particularly if you are relying on your investments for passive income (e.g., from dividends or interest payments). If you plan to use your portfolio for income in the future, you might choose to focus on more income-generating assets.

### 4. Understand the Importance of Tax Implications

Tax efficiency plays a crucial role in managing and growing your portfolio. Understanding how your investments are taxed can help you avoid unexpected tax burdens and make the most of your returns. Key considerations include:

Tax-Deferred Accounts: Investing through tax-advantaged accounts, such as IRAs or 401(k)s, can reduce the amount of tax you owe annually and allow your investments to grow without the tax burden until withdrawal.

Capital Gains Tax: Long-term capital gains (from investments held for more than a year) are generally taxed at a lower rate than short-term gains (from investments held for less than a year). Understanding how your investments are taxed can help you minimize tax liabilities.

**Tax-Efficient Funds:** Consider investing in tax-efficient mutual funds or exchange-traded funds (ETFs) that are designed to minimize taxable distributions. These funds usually focus on minimizing capital gains distributions, which can be a tax burden for investors in taxable accounts.

When to Buy, Hold, or Sell

Investors often face the dilemma of deciding when to buy, hold, or sell a particular investment. While there are no guarantees in the stock market, having a clear strategy can help you make more informed decisions. Let's explore these three key decisions:

**1. When to Buy**

Buying an investment is the first step in any successful portfolio. The key to buying an asset is identifying when it is undervalued and aligns with your investment strategy.

Some common factors to consider before purchasing an asset include:

**Valuation:** Buy stocks or assets when they are trading below their intrinsic value. Use fundamental analysis (e.g., P/E ratio, P/B ratio, etc.) to determine whether a stock is undervalued. You should also consider technical indicators like support and resistance levels to identify entry points.

**Alignment with Financial Goals:** Ensure that the investment aligns with your financial objectives. For example, if your goal is income generation, you might prioritize dividend-paying stocks, while if your goal is capital appreciation, you might focus on growth stocks.

**Market Timing:** While timing the market is difficult, it's essential to buy when market conditions are favorable. Buying during market dips or corrections can lead to significant long-term gains as prices recover.

## 2. When to Hold

Holding an investment means that you believe in its long-term potential, even if the market experiences short-term fluctuations. It's important to stick to your strategy and maintain patience. Here are some scenarios when holding an investment is the right decision:

**Strong Fundamentals:** If a company has strong financials, an attractive growth strategy, and a competitive advantage in its industry, it might be worth holding onto the stock even if the price temporarily declines.

**Long-Term Investment Horizon:** For investors with a long-term perspective, short-term market volatility should not result in panic selling. Holding an investment during market corrections can allow you to benefit from long-term growth when the market recovers.

**Reinvesting Dividends:** If your strategy includes dividend investing, holding onto dividend-paying stocks and reinvesting the dividends is a powerful way to compound returns over time.

### 3. When to Sell

Deciding when to sell can be one of the most difficult aspects of investing. Here are some scenarios when selling might be necessary:

**When Your Investment No Longer Aligns with Your Goals:** If the company or asset you've invested in no longer supports your financial goals, it might be time to sell. For example, if a growth stock no longer has potential for expansion or a dividend-paying stock cuts its dividend, it might no longer fit your strategy.

**Achieving a Target Return:** If your investment has reached your desired target price or has achieved the return you were hoping for, you might choose to sell and lock in profits. However, this should be done carefully, keeping in mind whether the stock still has room for further growth.

**Significant Changes in the Business or Industry:** If a company faces significant setbacks—such as declining market share, poor management decisions, or increasing competition—it might be time to sell. Similarly, if the industry faces regulatory changes that could negatively affect the company's long-term prospects, it might be prudent to sell.

### Rebalancing Strategies

Rebalancing is an essential component of managing your portfolio. As market conditions change, the proportions of various assets in your portfolio may shift, leading to an imbalance. Rebalancing ensures that your portfolio remains aligned with your investment goals, risk tolerance, and time horizon.

**1. What is Rebalancing?**

Rebalancing involves adjusting the asset allocation in your portfolio to maintain your desired risk level. For example, if one sector or asset class (e.g., tech stocks) outperforms and grows larger than planned, rebalancing ensures that you reduce your exposure to that sector and reinvest in other areas that may have underperformed.

**2. How Often Should You Rebalance?**

Rebalancing can be done either on a set schedule (e.g., annually, quarterly) or when your portfolio has shifted beyond a predetermined threshold (e.g., when any asset class exceeds or falls below a certain percentage of your portfolio). Some investors prefer to rebalance on a fixed schedule to avoid excessive trading, while others may use a threshold-based approach to take advantage of significant shifts in the market.

### 3. The Benefits of Rebalancing

**Rebalancing offers several key benefits:**

**Maintains Desired Risk Level:** Regular rebalancing helps to ensure that your portfolio remains aligned with your risk tolerance. For example, if stocks have performed exceptionally well, your portfolio may become riskier than originally intended. Rebalancing helps to bring it back to a balanced risk profile.

Locks in Profits: By selling assets that have appreciated significantly and buying assets that have underperformed, rebalancing helps you lock in profits and buy low.

**Avoids Overexposure:** Rebalancing ensures that no single investment or asset class dominates your portfolio, reducing the risk of significant losses in case of a market downturn.

Monitoring and adjusting your portfolio is an ongoing process that requires vigilance, discipline, and a long-term perspective. By regularly reviewing performance, staying informed about market trends, and making necessary adjustments, you can ensure that your portfolio remains in line with your financial goals and risk tolerance. The key decisions of when to buy, hold, or sell can significantly impact your returns, so it's essential to approach these decisions carefully and strategically. Rebalancing your portfolio regularly helps maintain its optimal composition, balancing risk and reward to maximize long-term growth.

# Chapter 13

## *Tax Implications of Investing*

Investing is an essential way to grow wealth, but it's also important to understand the tax implications that come with it. Taxes can significantly affect the returns on your investments, making it essential for investors to be aware of how different investment activities are taxed. By understanding key concepts like capital gains, losses, and tax-advantaged accounts, investors can make more informed decisions and optimize their investment strategies to minimize their tax liabilities. In this article, we will explore these topics in detail to help you navigate the complex landscape of investment taxes.

### 1. Understanding Capital Gains and Losses

Capital gains and losses are fundamental to understanding investment taxes. They play a pivotal role in determining how much tax you owe based on the profits or losses from the sale of investments. Here's a comprehensive breakdown of these concepts:

**Capital Gains**

Capital gains occur when you sell an investment for more than its original purchase price, resulting in a profit. These gains are taxed differently depending on how long you hold the investment before selling it.

**Short-Term Capital Gains:** If you sell an investment that you've held for one year or less, the profit is considered short-term capital gains and is taxed at your ordinary income tax rate. This means that the gains are subject to the same tax rate as your wages, interest income, and other earned income.

**Long-Term Capital Gains:** Investments held for more than one year are taxed at long-term capital gains rates, which are generally more favorable than short-term rates. For most individuals, long-term capital gains are taxed at a lower rate, often 0%, 15%, or 20%, depending on your income level. This is one of the reasons why long-term investing is often considered a tax-efficient strategy.

**The tax rates for long-term capital gains are structured based on your income:**

0%: For taxpayers in the 10% or 12% income

tax brackets.

15%: For those in the 22%, 24%, 32%, or 35% tax brackets.

20%: For taxpayers in the 37% tax bracket.

In some cases, certain types of capital gains—such as those from the sale of real estate or qualified small business stock—may be subject to additional tax incentives or exemptions.

## Capital Losses

Capital losses occur when you sell an investment for less than what you paid for it, resulting in a loss. While capital losses reduce your taxable income, they can also help offset capital gains and lower your overall tax liability. Here's how capital losses work:

**Offsetting Gains:** If you have both capital gains and losses in a given year, you can use your capital losses to offset the gains. For example, if you have $5,000 in capital gains from one investment but also incur $3,000 in capital losses from another, your net taxable capital gain will be reduced to $2,000.

**Tax-Loss Harvesting:** This strategy involves intentionally selling investments that are currently at a loss to offset taxable gains in the same year. It can help reduce your tax liability, particularly in years when you realize significant capital gains.

**Carrying Over Losses:** If your capital losses exceed your capital gains, you can use up to $3,000 of your net capital losses to offset ordinary income ($1,500 if married and filing separately). Any remaining losses can be carried forward to future tax years to offset gains or income.

### Net Investment Income Tax (NIIT)

In addition to regular capital gains taxes, higher-income individuals may also be subject to a 3.8% Net Investment Income Tax (NIIT) on certain investment income, including capital gains, dividends, and interest. The NIIT applies to individuals with a modified adjusted gross income (MAGI) exceeding $200,000 ($250,000 for married couples filing jointly).

**The NIIT is applied to the lesser of:**

Your net investment income.

The amount by which your MAGI exceeds

the applicable threshold.

For example, if you're a single filer with MAGI of $250,000, you could be subject to the NIIT on $50,000 of your net investment income, in addition to the regular capital gains tax.

## 2. Tax-Advantaged Accounts

Tax-advantaged accounts are specialized investment accounts that offer various tax benefits, helping investors minimize their tax liability and grow their wealth more efficiently. These accounts allow you to either defer taxes or avoid taxes on investment income altogether. Let's discuss some of the most common types of tax-advantaged accounts:

### Individual Retirement Accounts (IRAs)

An Individual Retirement Account (IRA) is a tax-advantaged account designed to help individuals save for retirement. IRAs come in two main types: Traditional IRAs and Roth IRAs, each offering distinct tax benefits.

**Traditional IRA:** Contributions to a traditional IRA are tax-deductible in the year they are made, which can reduce your taxable income for that year. However, taxes are due when you withdraw the funds in retirement. The tax rate on withdrawals depends on your income level at the time of withdrawal, but because the money grows tax-deferred, you have the potential to grow your investments without paying taxes during your working years.

**Contribution Limits:** For 2024, the contribution limit is $6,500 per year (or $7,500 if you're 50 or older).

**Required Minimum Distributions (RMDs):** Starting at age 73, you must begin withdrawing a minimum amount each year from your traditional IRA. These withdrawals are taxed as ordinary income.

**Roth IRA:** Roth IRAs work differently. Contributions to a Roth IRA are made with after-tax dollars, meaning you don't get an immediate tax deduction. However, your investments grow tax-free, and you can withdraw funds in retirement without paying taxes. This is particularly advantageous if you expect your income to be higher in retirement.

**Contribution Limits:** The contribution limit for a Roth IRA is the same as for a Traditional IRA. However, Roth IRAs have income limits that may prevent high earners from contributing directly.

No RMDs: Unlike Traditional IRAs, Roth IRAs do not require RMDs, allowing your funds to grow tax-free for as long as you like.

401(k) Plans

A 401(k) plan is an employer-sponsored retirement account that allows employees to save for retirement while receiving tax benefits. Like IRAs, 401(k)s offer two main types: Traditional 401(k) and Roth 401(k).

**Traditional 401(k):** Contributions to a Traditional 401(k) are made with pre-tax dollars, reducing your taxable income for the year. Taxes are paid upon withdrawal during retirement, at the individual's ordinary income tax rate.

**Contribution Limits:** For 2024, the contribution limit is $22,500 per year (or $30,000 if you're 50 or older).

**Employer Contributions:** Many employers match a portion of your contributions, making it a valuable retirement savings tool.

Roth 401(k): A Roth 401(k) allows employees to make after-tax contributions, meaning the contributions don't reduce your taxable income for the year. However, qualified withdrawals during retirement are tax-free, similar to a Roth IRA.

**Contribution Limits:** The contribution limits for Roth 401(k) are the same as Traditional 401(k) accounts.

### Health Savings Accounts (HSAs)

A Health Savings Account (HSA) is a tax-advantaged account that allows individuals to save for medical expenses. While it's not a traditional investment account, HSAs offer some of the most advantageous tax benefits available:

**Triple Tax Advantage:** Contributions to an HSA are tax-deductible, reducing your taxable income. The funds grow tax-free, and withdrawals for qualified medical expenses are also tax-free.

Contribution Limits: In 2024, the contribution limit is $3,850 for individuals and $7,750 for families. People aged 55 or older can contribute an additional $1,000 as a catch-up contribution.

No RMDs: Unlike retirement accounts, there are no required minimum distributions for

HSAs, meaning the funds can grow tax-free indefinitely.

529 College Savings Plans

A 529 College Savings Plan is a tax-advantaged account designed to help save for educational expenses. Contributions are made with after-tax dollars, but the investments grow tax-free, and withdrawals used for qualified educational expenses are also tax-free.

**Qualified Expenses:** Qualified expenses include tuition, fees, books, and room and board for college or other eligible educational institutions.

**Contribution Limits:** Contribution limits vary by state, but some states allow contributions of up to $300,000 per beneficiary. Each state has its own rules about the deductibility of contributions.

**State Tax Benefits:** Some states offer a tax deduction for contributions to a 529 plan, which can be a valuable benefit for residents.

The tax implications of investing are an essential consideration for anyone looking to build wealth. By understanding the nuances of capital gains and losses, and utilizing tax-advantaged accounts like IRAs, 401(k)s, and HSAs, investors can minimize their tax liabilities and maximize the growth potential of their investments. Careful planning and consideration of tax implications can help you develop a more efficient, long-term investment strategy and keep more of your hard-earned money working for you. Always consult with a tax professional or financial advisor to make sure your investment strategy aligns with your overall financial goals while optimizing your tax efficiency.

# Chapter 14

## *Mitigating Risks in Investing*

Investing in the stock market offers substantial opportunities for wealth accumulation, but it also carries inherent risks. As a result, managing and mitigating these risks is crucial for long-term success. While risk cannot be completely eliminated, investors can take various steps to minimize potential losses and protect their portfolios. In this article, we will discuss the different strategies available for mitigating investment risks, focusing on stop-loss orders, other protective measures, and hedging against market downturns.

### *1. Stop-Loss Orders and Other Protective Strategies*

Risk management tools, such as stop-loss orders and other protective strategies, are essential to minimizing potential losses in volatile market conditions. These strategies allow investors to set predetermined levels at which they will sell their investments to protect themselves from substantial declines. Let's explore these strategies in detail.

## Stop-Loss Orders

A stop-loss order is an automatic instruction to sell a security when its price falls to a specified level. The main goal of a stop-loss order is to limit the amount of loss an investor is willing to take on an investment. Here's how stop-loss orders work and why they are valuable:

**Definition and Mechanism:** A stop-loss order becomes a market order once the price of the security reaches or falls below the predetermined "stop price." For example, if you purchase a stock at $50 and set a stop-loss order at $45, your stock will automatically be sold if the price drops to $45. This can help prevent large losses if the market moves against you.

**Types of Stop-Loss Orders:**

**Standard Stop-Loss Order:** This is the simplest type of stop order, which turns into a market order once the stop price is triggered. The disadvantage of a standard stop-loss order is that in fast-moving markets, the stock may be sold at a price lower than the stop price due to slippage.

**Trailing Stop-Loss Order:** A trailing stop is a more advanced version that adjusts the stop price as the market price moves in your favor. For example, if you set a trailing stop order at $5 below the current price, and the stock rises from $50 to $55, your stop price will automatically adjust to $50. This allows you to lock in profits while still protecting against significant losses if the price reverses.

**Advantages:**

**Automatic Execution:** One of the key benefits of a stop-loss order is that it automatically triggers once the price reaches a specified level, eliminating the need for constant monitoring of the market.

**Minimizing Emotional Decisions:** By setting a predetermined stop price, investors can avoid the emotional decision-making that often leads to holding onto a losing position in the hope of a market rebound.

Protecting Gains: A stop-loss order allows investors to protect profits, particularly in volatile markets where prices can swing significantly.

**Disadvantages:**

**False Triggers:** In choppy or volatile markets, prices may briefly dip below the stop price, triggering a sale that could have been avoided if the market recovered quickly. This can lead to a sell-off at an inopportune time.

**Limited Control:** Because stop-loss orders often turn into market orders once triggered, the investor has no control over the price at which the security is sold, which can sometimes be lower than expected due to market fluctuations.

### Other Protective Strategies

In addition to stop-loss orders, several other protective strategies can help investors manage risk and protect their portfolios.

**Limit Orders:** A limit order is an instruction to buy or sell a stock at a specific price or better. For example, you might place a sell limit order at $50, ensuring that you will only sell the stock at that price or higher. Unlike stop-loss orders, limit orders are not designed to protect against losses, but they can help investors exit positions at favorable prices.

**Diversification:** One of the most effective ways to mitigate risk is through diversification. By spreading investments across different asset classes, sectors, and geographies, investors reduce the impact of a poor-performing investment on their overall portfolio. Diversification can help smooth returns over time and reduce the risk of large losses.

**Position Sizing:** Position sizing refers to determining the appropriate amount of capital to allocate to each individual investment based on the risk level and the investor's overall portfolio size. By limiting exposure to any single investment, investors can reduce the impact of potential losses from any one position.

**Asset Allocation:** Asset allocation is the process of dividing investments among different asset classes, such as stocks, bonds, real estate, and cash. By holding a mix of assets, investors can reduce the overall risk of their portfolio because different asset classes tend to perform differently under various market conditions.

**Risk Tolerance Assessment:** Understanding your own risk tolerance is critical for selecting the right protective strategies. Risk tolerance refers to the level of risk an investor is comfortable with. Assessing risk tolerance helps determine the appropriate mix of assets and the use of protective strategies, such as stop-loss orders or hedging, to avoid excessive losses.

## 2. Hedging Against Market Downturns

Hedging is a strategy used by investors to protect their portfolios from potential losses due to market declines. Hedging involves using financial instruments, such as options, futures, or inverse exchange-traded funds (ETFs), to offset the risks of adverse market movements. Here are some common methods of hedging against market downturns:

### Using Options for Hedging

Options are powerful financial instruments that allow investors to manage risk by providing the right, but not the obligation, to buy or sell a security at a predetermined price within a specific timeframe. Options can be used to hedge against downside risk in a portfolio.

**Put Options:** A put option gives the investor the right to sell an underlying asset at a predetermined price (the strike price) before a specified expiration date. If the price of the underlying asset declines, the value of the put option increases, offsetting the losses from the underlying asset. For example, if you hold shares in a company and are concerned about a potential decline in the stock price, you can purchase a put option to protect your position. If the stock falls, the gains from the put option can offset the losses from the stock.

**Covered Calls:** A covered call involves holding a long position in a stock and selling a call option on that same stock. This strategy allows you to generate additional income from the premiums received from selling the call option. While it doesn't directly protect against downturns, it can provide some downside protection by generating income to offset potential losses in the stock. However, the trade-off is that if the stock rises above the strike price, you may miss out on some of the upside.

**Collars:** A collar is a hedging strategy that combines buying a put option and selling a call option on the same asset. This creates a "protective band" around the stock's price, where the downside risk is limited by the put option, and the upside potential is capped by the call option. This strategy is commonly used by investors who want to protect their positions but are willing to give up some of the potential upside to achieve that protection.

## Inverse Exchange-Traded Funds (ETFs)

Inverse ETFs are designed to profit from a decline in the value of an underlying index or asset. These ETFs seek to deliver the opposite performance of the benchmark index they track. For example, if the S&P 500 declines by 1%, an inverse S&P 500 ETF will increase by approximately 1%. Inverse ETFs can be used to hedge against market downturns by taking short positions in the broader market or specific sectors.

**Leveraged Inverse ETFs:** Leveraged inverse ETFs take the concept of inverse ETFs a step further by using leverage to amplify returns. These ETFs aim to deliver a multiple of the inverse performance of the underlying index. For example, a 2x leveraged inverse ETF seeks to return twice the inverse performance of the benchmark index. While these ETFs can provide significant protection in a market downturn, they come with higher risk due to the use of leverage, and they are generally more suitable for short-term trading rather than long-term hedging.

## Futures Contracts

Futures contracts are standardized

agreements to buy or sell an underlying asset at a specific price on a future date. Futures contracts are commonly used by institutional investors and traders to hedge against price movements in commodities, stocks, and other financial assets.

**Hedging with Stock Index Futures:**
Investors can use stock index futures to hedge against a potential downturn in the stock market. By taking a short position in a futures contract, investors can profit from a decline in the index, offsetting the losses in their stock portfolio. Futures are highly leveraged instruments, meaning that small price movements can have a significant impact on the value of the contract, so they must be used cautiously.

**Risk Parity and Dynamic Hedging**

**Risk Parity:** Risk parity is an investment strategy that focuses on allocating risk rather than capital. The strategy seeks to balance the risk contribution of each asset class in the portfolio. By allocating more capital to lower-volatility assets like bonds and less to higher-risk assets like stocks, the risk parity approach aims to reduce the overall volatility of the portfolio and mitigate losses during market downturns.

**Dynamic Hedging:** Dynamic hedging involves adjusting the hedge based on changing market conditions. Investors using this strategy actively monitor their portfolio and modify their hedge positions based on market volatility, economic events, and other factors. The goal is to reduce downside risk while maintaining exposure to potential gains.

Mitigating risks is a critical aspect of successful investing, especially during periods of market volatility. Tools like stop-loss orders, diversification, and various hedging strategies can help investors limit their downside and protect their portfolios from substantial losses. While these strategies are not foolproof, they provide investors with valuable ways to reduce risk and make more informed decisions. Ultimately, a combination of protective strategies, proper asset allocation, and a clear understanding of risk tolerance can help investors navigate the complexities of the market while safeguarding their financial goals.

# Part 5: Advanced Strategies for Experienced Investors

## Chapter 15

### *Options and Derivatives*

Options and derivatives are sophisticated financial instruments that provide investors with a way to hedge risks, enhance returns, or speculate on the future movement of an asset. These instruments offer the flexibility to profit from both rising and falling markets, but they also carry significant risks. In this article, we will delve deeply into the basics of call and put options, as well as explore how options can be used to enhance returns. This guide is tailored to experienced investors who are looking to add these advanced strategies to their investment toolbox.

### 1. *Basics of Call and Put Options*

Options are contracts that give investors the right, but not the obligation, to buy or sell an underlying asset at a predetermined price before a specific expiration date. There are two main types of options: call options and put options. Understanding how each of these works is crucial to utilizing them in your investment strategy.

## Call Options

A call option is a financial contract that gives the buyer the right, but not the obligation, to buy a specific asset at a predetermined price, called the strike price, within a set time frame (before the option expires). Call options are typically purchased when an investor believes the price of the underlying asset will rise.

Example of a Call Option: Let's say you buy a call option for Stock XYZ with a strike price of $50 and an expiration date one month from now. If the stock price rises to $60 before the option expires, you can exercise your option to buy the stock at $50, even though it's now worth $60, yielding a profit of $10 per share (minus the premium paid for the option). If the stock price does not rise above $50, your only loss would be the premium paid for the option.

**Call Option Components:**

Strike Price: The price at which the underlying asset can be bought.

**Premium:** The price paid for the option.

Expiration Date: The date by which the option must be exercised.

**In the Money (ITM):** When the current price of the underlying asset is above the strike price for a call option.

**Out of the Money (OTM):** When the current price of the underlying asset is below the strike price for a call option.

**At the Money (ATM):** When the current price of the underlying asset is equal to the strike price.

**Advantages of Call Options:**

**Leverage:** Investors can control a large amount of stock with a relatively small investment (the premium). This offers potential for high returns if the asset's price moves significantly in the investor's favor.

**Limited Risk:** The maximum loss is limited to the premium paid for the option, making it a defined-risk strategy.

**Risks of Call Options:**

**Time Decay:** Options lose value as they approach expiration, especially if the underlying asset's price doesn't move in the anticipated direction.

**Premium Loss:** If the option expires without being exercised (i.e., the stock price does not rise above the strike price), the investor loses the entire premium paid for the option.

## Put Options

A put option is the opposite of a call option. It gives the buyer the right, but not the obligation, to sell an underlying asset at a predetermined price (strike price) before the option expires. Investors typically purchase put options when they expect the price of an asset to fall.

Example of a Put Option: Suppose you buy a put option for Stock XYZ with a strike price of $50. If the stock price falls to $40 before expiration, you can sell the stock at $50, even though it's now worth $40, securing a profit of $10 per share (minus the premium paid for the option). If the stock price stays above $50, the option expires worthless, and your loss is limited to the premium paid for the option.

**Put Option Components:**

**Strike Price:** The price at which the underlying asset can be sold.

**Premium:** The price paid for the option.

**Expiration Date:** The date by which the option must be exercised.

**In the Money (ITM):** When the current price of the underlying asset is below the strike price for a put option.

**Out of the Money (OTM):** When the current price of the underlying asset is above the strike price for a put option.

**At the Money (ATM):** When the current price of the underlying asset is equal to the strike price.

**Advantages of Put Options:**

Hedging: Put options can be used as a form of insurance to protect a portfolio from potential losses in a declining market.

**Profit in Falling Markets:** Just as call options profit from rising markets, put options allow investors to benefit from a market downturn.

**Risks of Put Options:**

**Premium Loss:** Like call options, if the stock price does not fall below the strike price, the investor loses the premium paid for the option.

**Time Decay:** Put options also suffer from time decay, meaning the option's value diminishes as it approaches expiration.

## 2. Using Options to Enhance Returns

While options provide opportunities to limit risk, they can also be used to enhance returns. Investors can use various strategies involving options to generate income, leverage their positions, and increase their overall returns. Below are a few key strategies for using options to enhance returns:

### Covered Calls

A covered call strategy involves owning a stock and selling a call option on that same stock. This strategy is typically used by investors who expect little movement in the price of the underlying asset or who are willing to cap their potential upside in exchange for additional income.

How It Works: Suppose you own 100 shares of Stock XYZ, which is currently trading at $50 per share. You sell a call option with a strike price of $55 and receive a premium of $3 per share. If the stock price rises above $55, the buyer of the call option will exercise their right to buy the stock from you at $55.

You still make a profit from the $55 sale price, plus the $3 premium you received for selling the option. However, if the stock price remains below $55, you keep the premium as income, and you continue to hold the stock.

**Advantages:**

**Income Generation:** By selling calls, you receive the premium upfront, which can add income to your portfolio.

**Limited Downside Risk:** If the stock declines in value, the premium received from selling the call helps offset the loss.

**Risks:**

**Capped Upside Potential:** If the stock rises above the strike price, your potential profit is limited to the strike price plus the premium received.

**Obligation to Sell:** If the stock is called away (i.e., the buyer exercises the call), you must sell the stock at the strike price, even if the stock continues to rise.

### Protective Puts

A protective put strategy involves buying put options on a stock you already own. This is essentially a form of insurance against a significant decline in the value of the stock. The goal is to limit downside risk while still participating in any potential upside.

**How It Works**: Suppose you own 100 shares of Stock XYZ, currently trading at $50 per share. You buy a put option with a strike price of $45. If the stock falls below $45, the put option increases in value, offsetting the losses in the stock. If the stock rises, your potential gains in the stock are not limited, but the cost of the put option (the premium) is a small expense.

**Advantages:**

**Downside Protection:** The protective put provides a safety net in case the stock price declines significantly.

**Unlimited Upside Potential:** Unlike covered calls, the protective put allows the stock to rise without capping your gains.

**Risks:**

**Premium Cost:** The cost of buying the put option is a consideration, and if the stock price doesn't decline, the premium paid for the put is a sunk cost.

**Potential Overpaying for Protection:** In volatile markets, put options can become expensive, making it harder to justify the protection if the stock doesn't experience a significant drop.

## Iron Condor

The iron condor is a popular options strategy that involves selling both a put and a call option, while simultaneously buying a put and a call option at different strike prices. This strategy profits from low volatility and is generally used when the investor believes the price of the underlying asset will stay within a certain range.

**How It Works:** An investor sells a put option with a strike price of $50 and a call option with a strike price of $60. At the same time, they buy a put option with a strike price of $45 and a call option with a strike price of $65. The premium received from selling the options exceeds the cost of buying the protective options, resulting in a net credit.

**Advantages:**

**Limited Risk:** The maximum loss is limited to the difference between the strike prices, minus the net credit received.

**Profit from Range-bound Markets:** The strategy profits if the underlying asset stays within a narrow range.

**Risks:**

**Limited Profit Potential:** The maximum profit is the net credit received, which can be relatively small compared to the potential loss.

**Complexity:** The strategy requires precise execution and careful monitoring, which can be difficult for novice traders.

Options and derivatives provide experienced investors with powerful tools to enhance returns and manage risk. While options can be complex, they offer significant opportunities to hedge, generate income, and leverage positions. By understanding the basics of call and put options and incorporating advanced strategies like covered calls, protective puts, and iron condors, investors can take advantage of market movements in ways that traditional investments may not allow.

However, it is essential to approach options with caution, as they carry substantial risks. Investors should carefully assess their risk tolerance, fully understand the mechanics of the options they trade, and continually educate themselves to master these advanced strategies. By doing so, they can unlock a broader array of tools to optimize their investment strategies and potentially increase their portfolio returns.

# Chapter 16

## *Short Selling Explained*

Short selling, or "shorting," is an advanced investment strategy in which an investor seeks to profit from a decline in the price of a stock or other asset. While this can be a powerful way to profit in bear markets, it carries substantial risks. It involves borrowing shares of a stock from a broker, selling them on the open market, and then buying them back later at a lower price to return to the broker.

In this detailed guide, we will explain how short selling works, the risks and rewards of betting against stocks, leveraging margin and borrowing, and the pros and cons of investing on margin. We will also discuss managing leverage effectively to minimize risks and maximize potential rewards.

## 1. *How Short Selling Works*

Short selling can be an appealing strategy when an investor believes that a stock is overvalued or that the market is headed for a downturn. The basic mechanics of short selling include the following steps:

**Step 1: Borrowing Shares:** The investor borrows shares of the stock they intend to short from a broker. The broker lends the shares from their inventory or from another investor's margin account. In exchange for borrowing the shares, the investor agrees to return them at a later date.

**Step 2: Selling the Shares:** The investor sells the borrowed shares in the open market at the current market price, hoping that the price of the stock will decline in the future.

**Step 3: Buying Back the Shares:** If the price of the stock falls, the investor buys the same number of shares back at the lower price.

**Step 4: Returning the Shares:** The investor returns the shares to the broker, keeping the difference between the price at which they sold the shares and the price at which they bought them back as profit.

For example, if an investor shorts 100 shares of a stock at $50 per share, they initially receive $5,000 from the sale. If the stock price falls to $40 per share, the investor can buy the shares back for $4,000, returning them to the broker and pocketing a profit of $1,000 (excluding transaction fees).

## 2. Risks and Rewards of Betting Against Stocks

Short selling offers unique opportunities but also presents substantial risks. Unlike buying stocks, where the maximum loss is limited to the amount invested, short selling has the potential for unlimited losses, making it one of the riskiest strategies in investing.

### Risks of Short Selling

Unlimited Losses: When you buy a stock, the worst-case scenario is that the stock's price drops to zero, and you lose your entire investment. In contrast, when you short a stock, the price can theoretically rise infinitely. If the stock price increases significantly, you will need to buy it back at a much higher price, resulting in a loss that can exceed your initial investment. The losses are potentially unlimited, and the investor must be prepared for the possibility that the price will keep rising.

**Margin Calls:** Short selling typically requires the use of margin, meaning that you borrow money to execute the trade. If the stock price rises, the broker may issue a margin call, requiring the investor to deposit more funds into their account to cover the losses. If the investor cannot meet the margin call, the broker may liquidate their position at a loss, further exacerbating the financial damage.

**Short Squeeze:** A short squeeze occurs when the price of a stock being shorted unexpectedly rises sharply, forcing short sellers to buy back shares to cover their positions. This, in turn, drives the stock price even higher, compounding the losses for short sellers. Short squeezes can be triggered by positive news about the company, a change in market sentiment, or a large institutional investor buying up the stock.

**Borrowing Costs:** Borrowing shares to short is not free. Investors are required to pay fees to the broker for borrowing the shares, which can increase the cost of short selling. Additionally, if the stock becomes difficult to borrow (e.g., if a lot of other investors are shorting it), borrowing costs can rise significantly, further eroding the potential for profit.

## Rewards of Short Selling

**Profiting from Declines:** Short selling offers the opportunity to profit from market declines. In a bear market or during a stock price correction, shorting overvalued stocks can yield significant returns.

**Hedging:** Investors can use short selling as a hedge against potential losses in their long positions. By shorting stocks that are correlated with their existing investments, investors can offset some of the losses from market downturns.

**Leverage:** Short selling provides leverage, as investors can control a larger position with a smaller amount of capital. This magnifies both potential profits and losses. When successful, the return on short selling can be substantial, as it allows investors to take advantage of price declines without having to own the stock.

**Market Inefficiencies:** In some cases, short selling can help correct market inefficiencies. When a stock is overvalued, short sellers can help drive the price down to its true value, promoting market efficiency.

## 3. Leveraging Margin and Borrowing

Leverage is a core component of short selling and can significantly increase both risk and reward. When you short sell, you are borrowing shares from a broker, and to do so, you must use margin. Margin is essentially a loan from your broker that allows you to increase the size of your position.

### Understanding Margin Accounts

A margin account is a brokerage account that allows investors to borrow money or assets from the broker to purchase securities. In the case of short selling, investors borrow shares of a stock, sell them in the market, and use the proceeds to meet the margin requirements set by the broker.

**Initial Margin Requirement:** This is the amount of equity (cash or securities) that an investor must deposit into their margin account to open a short position. This typically ranges from 50% to 100% of the value of the short sale.

**Maintenance Margin:** This is the minimum equity that must be maintained in the margin account after the short sale. If the equity in the account falls below this level, a margin call is triggered, and the investor must deposit additional funds or sell other securities to meet the requirement.

## Pros and Cons of Investing on Margin

Investing on margin allows investors to amplify their potential returns, but it also increases the risks involved. Let's break down the advantages and disadvantages of margin investing.

### Pros of Margin Investing

Increased Buying Power: Margin allows investors to control a larger position than they could with their own capital alone. This means they can make more significant investments and potentially earn higher returns.

**Leverage for Short Selling:** Margin accounts provide the ability to short sell, which is not possible in a regular cash account. Leverage allows short sellers to profit from declining markets.

**Diversification:** By using margin to increase their buying power, investors can diversify their portfolios without needing to raise additional funds.

### Cons of Margin Investing

Interest on Borrowed Funds: Investors who borrow funds on margin must pay interest on the amount borrowed. This can significantly erode profits, especially if the investment does not perform well.

**Risk of Margin Calls:** If the value of the investment declines and the margin account falls below the maintenance margin, the broker can issue a margin call, requiring the investor to deposit more funds. If the investor is unable to meet the margin call, the broker may sell the investor's securities to recover the loan, often at a loss.

**Amplified Losses:** Just as margin amplifies potential gains, it also amplifies potential losses. A small loss can turn into a large loss if the investor is using leverage.

**Forced Liquidation:** If an investor fails to meet a margin call, the broker may liquidate their position without the investor's consent, often locking in a loss.

### 4. Managing Leverage Effectively

Leverage can be a useful tool for experienced investors, but it requires careful management to minimize risks. Below are

**strategies for managing leverage effectively:**

**1. Maintain Adequate Cash Reserves**

One of the most important ways to manage leverage is by maintaining adequate cash reserves. This ensures that you can meet margin calls without being forced to sell other investments at a loss. Investors should avoid using excessive margin that could lead to liquidation in the event of a market downturn.

**2. Diversify Positions**

Leverage should not be concentrated in one or two positions. By diversifying investments across different asset classes or sectors, investors can reduce the risk of significant losses from any single position. Diversification helps to spread the risk and can prevent a margin call from wiping out the entire portfolio.

**3. Use Stop-Loss Orders**

Stop-loss orders are a vital tool for managing leverage. A stop-loss order automatically sells a security when its price falls to a predetermined level, limiting potential losses. By setting stop-loss orders for leveraged positions, investors can protect themselves from significant downturns.

### 4. Regularly Monitor Margin Levels

Leverage requires continuous monitoring. Investors should regularly review their margin levels to ensure they are not at risk of a margin call. If the value of an investment is declining, it may be wise to reduce leverage by selling a portion of the position before a margin call occurs.

### 5. Set Clear Exit Strategies

Having a clear exit strategy is essential for managing leveraged positions. Investors should define specific price targets at which they will take profits or cut losses. This helps to maintain discipline and prevents emotions from driving investment decisions.

### 6. Use Leverage Conservatively

While leverage can be enticing, it should be used conservatively, particularly in volatile markets. Investors should use leverage sparingly and avoid using it to speculate on high-risk positions. Leverage is most effective when used with a well-thought-out strategy and a clear understanding of the risks involved.

Short selling is a powerful strategy that can yield significant profits, but it comes with substantial risks. By understanding the mechanics of short selling, assessing the risks and rewards, and carefully managing margin and leverage, investors can use this strategy to enhance their portfolios.

However, short selling should not be taken lightly. It requires a high level of skill, discipline, and an understanding of the potential pitfalls. As with any advanced investment strategy, investors should only use short selling if they are confident in their knowledge and ability to manage the risks involved. With careful management, short selling can be an effective tool for profiting from market declines and hedging against potential losses.

# Chapter 17

## *Sector and Thematic Investing*

Sector and thematic investing are strategies that allow investors to target specific industries or themes within the economy that they believe will outperform over a certain period. While sector investing focuses on broad economic sectors, thematic investing hones in on specific trends or disruptive innovations that may reshape the future. Both of these strategies allow investors to capitalize on growth opportunities, but they come with their own set of risks and challenges.

In this article, we will explore sector and thematic investing in-depth, highlighting opportunities in emerging industries and the growing trend of Environmental, Social, and Governance (ESG) investing. We will discuss how to identify opportunities, assess risk, and understand how these strategies work in real-world applications.

### 1. Sector Investing: A Broader Approach

Sector investing involves dividing the economy into broad sectors and choosing to invest in specific sectors that are expected to perform well. This strategy focuses on the overall performance of a sector, typically through exchange-traded funds (ETFs), mutual funds, or individual stocks within the sector.

**Understanding the Major Sectors of the Economy**

Most economies can be broadly divided into several key sectors. These sectors include:

**Technology:** Includes companies involved in software, hardware, artificial intelligence (AI), cloud computing, cybersecurity, and more. This sector has seen explosive growth in recent decades and continues to be a primary driver of innovation.

**Healthcare:** Comprises pharmaceutical companies, biotechnology firms, healthcare providers, and medical equipment manufacturers. With an aging global population, the healthcare sector has long-term growth potential.

Financials: Includes banks, investment firms, insurance companies, and real estate investment trusts (REITs). The performance of financial stocks is closely tied to interest rates, economic conditions, and investor sentiment.

**Consumer Discretionary:** This sector includes companies that produce non-essential goods and services, such as entertainment, leisure, retail, and luxury products. This sector tends to perform well during periods of economic expansion.

**Consumer Staples:** Consists of companies that produce essential goods, such as food, beverages, and household products. These stocks tend to be more stable and defensive during economic downturns.

**Energy:** Includes companies involved in the production and distribution of energy resources, such as oil, gas, and renewable energy. The energy sector can be volatile, influenced by global supply and demand factors, geopolitical events, and environmental concerns.

**Utilities:** Covers industries such as electricity, water, and natural gas. Utility companies tend to provide stable, reliable returns due to their essential nature, and they are often seen as defensive investments.

**Industrials:** Includes companies involved in manufacturing, construction, transportation, and aerospace. This sector is sensitive to the economic cycle and often correlates with infrastructure development and economic growth.

**Materials:** Covers industries involved in the extraction and processing of natural resources, such as metals, chemicals, and construction materials. This sector often benefits from economic expansion and increased demand for raw materials.

**Real Estate:** Includes residential, commercial, and industrial properties, as well as real estate investment trusts (REITs). The performance of this sector is influenced by interest rates, economic conditions, and population growth.

### Opportunities in Emerging Sectors

Emerging sectors often provide the most compelling opportunities for growth. These sectors may not be as well established as the traditional ones but have the potential for significant upside as new technologies, trends, and markets develop. Some of the most exciting emerging sectors include:

**Renewable Energy:** As global efforts to combat climate change intensify, renewable energy is rapidly becoming one of the most important sectors of the economy. Solar, wind, and battery storage technologies are seeing massive investments. Governments and corporations are increasingly committing to net-zero emissions goals, creating long-term demand for clean energy solutions.

**Artificial Intelligence (AI) and Automation:** AI and automation are transforming industries across the board, from manufacturing to healthcare to finance. Companies that are developing AI-powered solutions or automating their processes are likely to see significant growth as adoption rates increase.

**Electric Vehicles (EVs):** With growing concerns about climate change and air pollution, the EV market is expanding rapidly. Companies involved in EV production, battery technology, charging infrastructure, and EV-related services are attracting significant investment.

**Biotechnology and Genomics:** Advances in genomics, personalized medicine, and biotechnology have the potential to revolutionize healthcare. Companies working on gene editing, cancer therapies, and regenerative medicine could see rapid growth in the coming years.

**Cybersecurity:** As more data moves online and cyber threats grow in complexity and frequency, cybersecurity is becoming increasingly important. Companies that provide security solutions for individuals, businesses, and governments are well-positioned for future growth.

## 2. Thematic Investing: Capitalizing on Trends

Thematic investing focuses on identifying long-term trends or themes that could disrupt entire industries or create new ones. These themes could involve technological innovations, social movements, or demographic shifts. Thematic investing is often more focused than sector investing, as it targets specific areas of the economy that are expected to outperform over time.

### How Thematic Investing Works

Thematic investing typically involves choosing a theme—such as clean energy, artificial intelligence, or digital transformation—and investing in companies that are directly or indirectly involved in that theme. Investors may choose ETFs or mutual funds that track a specific theme, or they may invest directly in individual stocks that are aligned with the theme.

Some of the most popular themes in thematic investing include:

**Sustainability and Green Investments:** As awareness of climate change and environmental issues grows, investors are increasingly turning to companies that focus on sustainability. This can include renewable energy companies, green building materials, electric vehicles, and companies with strong environmental, social, and governance (ESG) practices.

**Technological Disruption:** Technologies like AI, blockchain, quantum computing, and 5G are transforming industries. Thematic investors target companies that are developing or adopting these cutting-edge technologies, believing that these innovations will drive growth in the years to come.

**Aging Population:** As the global population ages, investors may choose to invest in companies that provide products or services to older adults, such as healthcare, home care, pharmaceuticals, and retirement planning.

**Digital Transformation:** With more businesses shifting to the digital space, investors may target companies involved in e-commerce, cloud computing, fintech, and digital infrastructure. Digital transformation is occurring across all sectors, and thematic investors seek to profit from this ongoing shift.

**Health and Wellness:** The rise of health-conscious living has led to an explosion in wellness-focused industries. This includes companies involved in fitness, organic foods, mental health, and wellness technology.

### Benefits and Risks of Thematic Investing

Thematic investing offers several benefits, but it also comes with unique risks. Some of the benefits include:

**High Growth Potential:** Thematic investing allows investors to capitalize on emerging trends that could lead to rapid growth. By identifying the right themes, investors can position themselves to benefit from disruptive changes.

**Focused Exposure to Trends:** Unlike sector investing, thematic investing gives investors targeted exposure to specific trends. This allows for more precise investment strategies and the ability to gain from niche opportunities.

**Diversification Across Sectors:** While thematic investing focuses on a particular trend, it can provide diversification across multiple sectors. For example, the digital transformation theme could include companies in software, hardware, and telecommunications.

**However, thematic investing also carries risks:**

**Volatility:** Themes, especially new and emerging ones, can experience high levels of volatility. Trends may take longer to develop than anticipated, or new competitors may disrupt the market.

**Lack of Historical Data:** Because thematic investing focuses on emerging trends, there may be limited historical data to evaluate the performance of these themes over time. This can make it difficult to assess the risks involved.

**Overexposure:** By focusing too heavily on one theme, investors may become overly concentrated in a single area. This can expose them to higher levels of risk if the theme underperforms or fails to materialize.

### 3. ESG Investing: Aligning Profit with Purpose

Environmental, Social, and Governance (ESG) investing is a strategy that focuses on selecting investments based on their adherence to ethical and sustainable practices. ESG investing has gained tremendous popularity over the last decade, driven by growing concerns about climate change, social justice, and corporate accountability.

### What is ESG Investing?

ESG investing involves evaluating companies based on three primary factors:

Environmental: This factor examines how a company manages its environmental impact, including its carbon footprint, waste management, energy consumption, and sustainability initiatives. Companies that prioritize green energy, reduce pollution, and mitigate climate change are considered more favorable.

**Social:** The social component focuses on a company's relationship with its employees, customers, suppliers, and communities. It includes issues such as labor practices, diversity and inclusion, product safety, and corporate social responsibility (CSR).

**Governance:** Governance refers to how a company is managed and includes aspects such as executive compensation, shareholder rights, and transparency. Companies with strong corporate governance are less likely to engage in fraudulent activities or suffer from internal conflicts.

### Opportunities in ESG Investing

**ESG investing presents several opportunities for investors:**

**Attractive Long-Term Growth:** Many ESG-compliant companies are seen as better managed and more resilient in the long run. As sustainability becomes increasingly important to consumers and investors, these companies are well-positioned for future growth.

**Attracting Capital:** There is a growing demand for socially responsible investments. ESG investing allows companies with strong ESG practices to attract capital from a wide array of investors who prioritize ethical investing.

**Lower Risk:** ESG-focused companies are often better at managing risk. By considering environmental, social, and governance factors, these companies are better equipped to address regulatory changes, public sentiment, and unforeseen disruptions.

### Challenges of ESG Investing

While ESG investing presents numerous opportunities, it also has its challenges:

**Lack of Standardization:** There is no universal definition of what constitutes ESG compliance. Different investment firms, analysts, and rating agencies may use different criteria to evaluate companies, making it difficult to compare investment options.

**Greenwashing:** Some companies may falsely claim to adhere to ESG standards to attract investment, a practice known as "greenwashing." This can mislead investors who are genuinely seeking to align their investments with their values.

**Potential Trade-Offs:** While ESG companies may be more resilient and profitable in the long term, they may not always provide the highest short-term returns. ESG investing may require patience and a longer-term perspective.

Sector and thematic investing represent two powerful strategies for investors looking to target specific industries or trends that offer growth potential. While sector investing provides a broader approach to the economy, thematic investing offers more targeted opportunities to capitalize on disruptive trends and innovations.

ESG investing further expands these strategies by aligning profit with purpose, allowing investors to support companies that prioritize sustainability, social responsibility, and strong governance. As these strategies continue to grow in popularity, they present unique opportunities and challenges for investors seeking to diversify their portfolios and invest in the future.

By understanding the opportunities, risks, and practical application of sector, thematic, and ESG investing, investors can build more focused, strategic portfolios that align with their financial goals and values.

# Chapter 18

## *The Power of Compounding: Maximizing Long-Term Returns and Real-Life Success Stories*

Compounding is often described as one of the most powerful forces in investing, capable of transforming modest investments into substantial fortunes over time. The beauty of compounding lies in its ability to generate returns not only on the original principal but also on the accumulated interest or earnings. Understanding the power of compounding can drastically change an investor's approach to wealth building, especially when considering long-term investments.

In this article, we will delve into how to maximize long-term returns through compounding and explore real-life examples of compounding success. We'll break down the key principles of compounding, examine the role of time in the investment process, and provide practical strategies for leveraging compounding to build significant wealth over time.

### 1. Understanding Compounding: The Basic Concept

At its core, compounding refers to the process of earning interest on both your initial investment (the principal) and the returns that accumulate over time. This creates a snowball effect where your money starts to work for you, earning money on money, and this accelerated growth becomes exponentially more powerful the longer your investment is allowed to grow.

To understand how compounding works, let's look at a simple example:

Initial Investment: Suppose you invest $1,000 in an account that offers a 5% annual interest rate.

Year 1: At the end of the first year, you earn $50 (5% of $1,000), so your total balance becomes $1,050.

Year 2: The next year, you earn 5% not on the original $1,000, but on the new balance of $1,050. This means you earn $52.50 (5% of $1,050), and your new balance is $1,102.50.

As you can see, over time, the returns start to increase at an accelerating rate because the interest earned in previous periods is added to the principal, thus earning more interest in the next period. This effect grows exponentially, and the longer the time period, the more powerful compounding becomes.

## 2. How to Maximize Long-Term Returns Through Compounding

To fully leverage the power of compounding, investors need to follow several key strategies that maximize long-term returns. Here are the most effective ways to achieve this:

**a) Start Early:** Time is Your Greatest Ally

The most important factor in maximizing the power of compounding is time. The earlier you start investing, the more time your investments have to grow and compound. Even small investments, if given enough time, can result in large amounts due to the exponential nature of compounding.

Example: Imagine two investors—one who begins investing $200 per month at age 25 and another who starts at age 35, contributing the same amount. Even if both investors stop contributing at age 65, the person who started investing at 25 will likely accumulate a significantly larger amount, simply due to the extra 10 years of compounding.

In investing, time allows your returns to compound continuously, creating a cumulative effect that accelerates as the years go by. This is why it's often said that the best time to start investing was yesterday, and the second best time is today.

**b) Reinvest Your Earnings**

Reinvesting the earnings from your investments is a critical strategy for maximizing compounding. Instead of taking your interest, dividends, or capital gains as cash, reinvest them back into the investment. This increases the size of your principal, leading to more substantial returns in the future.

Dividends: For example, if you invest in dividend-paying stocks, instead of cashing out the dividends, reinvest them by purchasing more shares of the stock. Over time, these additional shares will also begin to generate dividends, creating a larger pool of compounding returns.

Interest Income: Similarly, if you invest in bonds or savings accounts that pay interest, reinvesting that interest back into the same or similar interest-bearing assets helps amplify your investment.

The key to reinvesting successfully is consistency. The more often you reinvest, the faster your investments will grow. Whether you're reinvesting dividends, interest, or any other type of earnings, your returns will compound on a larger base, leading to significant wealth accumulation over time.

### c) Choose Investments with High Growth Potential

Not all investments are created equal when it comes to compounding. Some investments offer higher returns, which means that your principal will grow faster. High-growth investments, such as stocks, real estate, or certain types of mutual funds and exchange-traded funds (ETFs), tend to offer higher returns, which accelerate the compounding process.

**Stocks:** Historically, stocks have provided an average return of around 7-10% annually when accounting for dividends and capital gains. By investing in stocks with high growth potential, you can take advantage of these returns over the long term.

**Real Estate:** Real estate, particularly rental properties, can provide strong returns through both appreciation and rental income. Additionally, rental income can be reinvested in new properties, leading to further compounding of wealth.

**Mutual Funds and ETFs:** These vehicles often offer a diversified portfolio of stocks or bonds that can provide consistent returns. By reinvesting the dividends or capital gains, investors can compound their wealth steadily over time.

### d) Maintain a Long-Term Focus

Compounding works best when you allow your investments to grow over a long period without interruption. Short-term market fluctuations may cause anxiety for many investors, but the power of compounding relies on a long-term focus. This means avoiding the temptation to sell investments in response to market volatility.

**Staying Invested:** Even during market downturns, it's important to stay invested and continue to let your money compound. For instance, if you invest in stocks during a market dip and hold those stocks for the long term, you may see the value of your investments rise significantly over the years.

**Consistency:** Consistency in investing, regardless of short-term market conditions, is crucial for successful compounding. By regularly investing and reinvesting your returns, you ensure that your wealth continues to grow, even when the market isn't performing well.

### e) Use Tax-Advantaged Accounts

Certain investment accounts, like 401(k)s, IRAs, and other tax-advantaged accounts, allow for tax-deferred or tax-free growth, which can significantly enhance the compounding effect. By using these accounts, you can reinvest the full amount of your returns without having to pay taxes on them until later.

Example: In a Roth IRA, the money you contribute grows tax-free, and when you withdraw it in retirement, you don't owe any taxes. This allows your money to compound without the drag of taxes, accelerating the growth of your wealth.

### 3. Real-Life Examples of Compounding Success

To truly understand the power of

compounding, let's examine a few real-life examples of how compounding has helped investors build significant wealth over time.

Example 1: Warren Buffett's Wealth

Warren Buffett, one of the wealthiest individuals in the world, is often cited as a prime example of how compounding can create massive wealth. Buffett started investing at a young age, buying his first stock at age 11. Over decades of consistent investing in undervalued companies, Buffett's wealth grew substantially, largely due to the power of compounding.

**The Key to Buffett's Success:** One of Buffett's key principles is the idea of "buying good companies and holding them for the long term." The reinvestment of dividends, along with the continued growth of his investments, allowed his wealth to compound at an extraordinary rate. Buffett's net worth, which exceeds $100 billion, is a direct result of compounding over decades.

Example 2: The Power of Starting Early (The Tale of John and Mary)

Consider the following scenario: John and Mary both invest $5,000 a year in the stock market. John starts investing at age 25, while Mary waits until age 35. Both invest for 30 years, with an average annual return of 7%. Here's what happens:

**John's Investment:** After 30 years of consistent investing, John has contributed a total of $150,000 ($5,000 per year for 30 years). His total investment grows to about $1.25 million, thanks to the power of compounding.

**Mary's Investment:** Mary, who started investing 10 years later, contributed a total of $150,000 as well. However, due to the 10 years of lost compounding, her investment grows to only around $850,000.

This scenario shows that the earlier you start investing, the more time your investments have to compound. Even if both investors contributed the same amount, John's investments grew significantly more because of the additional 10 years of compounding.

Example 3: The Story of a $1,000 Investment Growing to $1 Million

Let's say an investor made a one-time investment of $1,000 in an index fund that tracks the S&P 500, which has historically returned about 10% per year. If that investor left the investment untouched for 50 years, it would grow as follows:

Initial Investment: $1,000

Annual Return: 10%

Investment Period: 50 years

By the end of 50 years, that $1,000 would have grown to over $1,000,000. This is the true magic of compounding—allowing a small investment to grow into a large sum over time with no additional contributions.

## Harnessing the Full Potential of Compounding

The power of compounding is a simple yet extraordinary force in investing. By starting early, reinvesting earnings, choosing high-growth investments, maintaining a long-term focus, and using tax-advantaged accounts, investors can maximize the compounding effect and build substantial wealth over time.

Through real-life examples such as Warren Buffett's success and the story of John and Mary, we can see that compounding works best when investments are left to grow without interruption. Time, patience, and consistency are the keys to turning modest investments into significant fortunes.

If you understand and apply the principles of compounding, you can unlock the full potential of your investments and set yourself on the path to financial success. The earlier you start, the more powerful compounding becomes—so take action today to build the wealth of tomorrow.

# Chapter 19

## Lessons from Successful Investors: Case Studies of Market Titans and Key Takeaways for Individual Investors

The world of investing has been shaped by individuals whose strategic insights, disciplined approaches, and groundbreaking philosophies have redefined success. From Warren Buffett's value investing principles to Ray Dalio's systematic risk management, studying the journeys of market titans provides invaluable lessons for individual investors. By dissecting their decisions, strategies, and thought processes, we can identify actionable takeaways that align with diverse investment goals.

This article delves into the case studies of some of the most successful investors and distills key lessons that can empower individual investors to navigate the financial markets effectively.

Part 1: Case Studies of Market Titans

1. Warren Buffett: The Oracle of Omaha

Investment Philosophy:

Warren Buffett, widely regarded as one of

the greatest investors of all time, is synonymous with value investing. His approach centers on identifying undervalued companies with strong fundamentals, competent management, and long-term growth potential. He famously said, "Price is what you pay; value is what you get."

### Notable Investment Examples:

**Coca-Cola:** Buffett's investment in Coca-Cola during the late 1980s remains a hallmark of his strategy. He recognized the company's global brand power, consistent earnings, and ability to generate cash flow. Despite short-term market fluctuations, he held onto the stock, which has since provided consistent dividends and capital appreciation.

**American Express:** Buffett invested in American Express during a period of financial turmoil in the 1960s. He saw beyond the immediate challenges and focused on the company's competitive advantage and loyal customer base. This decision paid off handsomely in the long run.

### Key Lessons:

**Focus on Intrinsic Value:** Identify stocks

trading below their intrinsic value and hold them until the market recognizes their true worth.

**Long-Term Perspective:** Patience is a virtue. Avoid being swayed by short-term market movements.

**Invest in What You Understand:** Buffett advocates for investing in industries and businesses that you can analyze and comprehend.

**2. Peter Lynch:** Master of Growth Investing

**Investment Philosophy:**

Peter Lynch, the legendary manager of the Fidelity Magellan Fund, achieved an average annual return of 29% during his tenure. His strategy revolved around identifying growth opportunities in industries and companies he understood. Lynch popularized the concept of "invest in what you know," encouraging investors to leverage their personal experiences when selecting stocks.

**Notable Investment Examples:**

**L'eggs (Hanesbrands):** Lynch noticed the popularity of L'eggs pantyhose among consumers and used this insight to invest in its parent company, Hanesbrands, before the stock's value soared.

**Dunkin' Donuts:** Observing the consistent popularity of Dunkin' Donuts' coffee and food offerings, Lynch invested early, benefiting from the company's subsequent growth.

**Key Lessons:**

**Do Your Homework:** Thoroughly research a company's fundamentals before investing.

**Identify Growth Catalysts:** Look for companies with strong earnings growth potential and competitive advantages.

Keep It Simple: Avoid overcomplicating your investment strategy; focus on straightforward, profitable businesses.

### 3. Ray Dalio: The Bridgewater Approach

**Investment Philosophy:**

Ray Dalio, the founder of Bridgewater Associates, is known for his principles-based approach to investing. Dalio emphasizes diversification and risk management, advocating for the creation of an "all-weather portfolio" that performs well across economic cycles. His strategy relies heavily on macroeconomic analysis and systematic decision-making.

**Notable Investment Examples:**

**Risk Parity Strategy:** Dalio's risk parity approach involves balancing investments across asset classes to achieve stable returns, regardless of market conditions. This strategy has been a cornerstone of Bridgewater's success.

**Global Diversification:** Dalio's investments span global markets, reducing dependency on any single region or sector.

**Key Lessons:**

**Diversification is Key:** Spread your investments across different asset classes and geographies to mitigate risk.

**Systematic Investing:** Develop a rules-based approach to investing that minimizes emotional decision-making.

**Understand Economic Trends:** Stay informed about macroeconomic factors that influence market movements.

**4. Cathie Wood:** Innovation and Disruption

**Investment Philosophy:**

Cathie Wood, the CEO of ARK Invest, is known for her focus on disruptive innovation. Her strategy targets companies leading advancements in technology, healthcare, and renewable energy. Wood takes a high-conviction approach, investing heavily in a select group of companies poised for exponential growth.

**Notable Investment Examples:**

Tesla: Wood was an early advocate of Tesla, recognizing its potential to revolutionize the automotive and energy industries. Her bullish stance paid off as Tesla's stock price soared.

Roku: She identified Roku's potential in the streaming industry before it became a dominant player.

Key Lessons:

**Embrace Innovation:** Don't shy away from investing in cutting-edge industries with high growth potential.

**High Conviction Pays Off:** Concentrate your investments in companies you deeply believe in.

**Stay Ahead of Trends:** Anticipate future

trends and invest accordingly.

Part 2: Key Takeaways for Individual Investors

1. Develop a Clear Investment Philosophy

Successful investors have a well-defined investment philosophy that guides their decisions. Whether it's value investing, growth investing, or a focus on innovation, having a clear framework ensures consistency and helps avoid impulsive decisions.

**2. Patience is Crucial**

One of the most common traits among successful investors is patience. Long-term investing allows the power of compounding to work its magic and reduces the impact of short-term volatility.

**3. Conduct Thorough Research**

Investing without research is akin to gambling. Before investing in any asset, understand its fundamentals, competitive position, growth prospects, and potential risks.

### 4. Diversify to Manage Risk

Diversification is essential for mitigating risk. Spread your investments across asset classes, industries, and geographies to protect your portfolio from market downturns.

### 5. Learn from Mistakes

Even the best investors make mistakes. What sets them apart is their ability to learn from those mistakes and refine their strategies. Treat every loss as a lesson.

### 6. Stay Informed

The financial markets are influenced by a myriad of factors, including economic trends, political developments, and technological advancements. Stay informed to make well-informed decisions.

### 7. Avoid Emotional Investing

Emotions like fear and greed can lead to irrational decisions. Develop a disciplined, rules-based approach to investing that minimizes emotional interference.

### 8. Leverage Compounding

The earlier you start investing, the more

time your investments have to compound. Reinvest dividends and earnings to maximize long-term returns.

The journeys of market titans like Warren Buffett, Peter Lynch, Ray Dalio, and Cathie Wood offer invaluable insights into the art and science of investing. While each investor employs a unique strategy, common themes such as discipline, patience, and thorough research emerge across their approaches.

For individual investors, the key lies in understanding your financial goals, risk tolerance, and investment horizon. By adopting proven strategies and avoiding common pitfalls, you can navigate the complexities of the market and build a robust portfolio. Remember, successful investing is a marathon, not a sprint—take the lessons from these icons and chart your path to financial success.

# Chapter 20

## Creating a Legacy Through, Investing: Passing Wealth to the Next Generation and the Role of Philanthropy in Financial Planning

Investing isn't solely about generating wealth for personal fulfillment; it's also about creating a lasting impact that transcends generations. Legacy-building involves planning and acting intentionally to ensure that wealth is not only preserved but also used to benefit future generations and society at large. This process encompasses financial education, estate planning, philanthropy, and a long-term vision for wealth management.

This article delves into the critical aspects of creating a legacy through investing, focusing on passing wealth to the next generation and integrating philanthropy into financial planning.

Part 1: Passing Wealth to the Next Generation

### 1. Building Generational Wealth

Generational wealth refers to assets passed down from one generation to the next, including investments, real estate, businesses, and intellectual capital. Creating and preserving this wealth requires strategic planning and foresight.

## Key Strategies for Building Generational Wealth

**Start Early:** The earlier you start investing, the more time your assets have to grow through the power of compounding. This creates a larger financial base to pass on.

**Diversify Investments:** Build a diversified portfolio that includes stocks, bonds, real estate, and other assets to mitigate risk and ensure long-term growth.

**Leverage Tax-Advantaged Accounts:** Utilize accounts like IRAs, 401(k)s, and other tax-advantaged vehicles to maximize returns and minimize tax liabilities.

## The Importance of Financial Literacy

One of the most critical aspects of passing wealth is equipping heirs with the knowledge and skills needed to manage it. Financial literacy empowers the next generation to make informed decisions, preventing the mismanagement of inherited wealth.

**Steps to Foster Financial Literacy:**

Begin with foundational concepts like budgeting, saving, and the basics of investing.

Encourage involvement in family financial discussions to expose younger generations to real-world scenarios.

Recommend reading materials, courses, or mentorships to deepen their understanding.

**2. Estate Planning:** The Blueprint for Legacy Transfer

Estate planning ensures that your assets are distributed according to your wishes while minimizing taxes and legal complexities.

**Key Components of Estate Planning**

Will: A legally binding document outlining how your assets should be distributed.

Trusts: Tools like revocable living trusts or irrevocable trusts can offer greater control over how assets are managed and distributed.

**Power of Attorney:** Designating someone to make financial or medical decisions on your behalf in case of incapacity.

**Beneficiary Designations:** Ensuring retirement accounts, life insurance policies, and other assets have up-to-date beneficiary designations.

### Minimizing Tax Implications

Estate and inheritance taxes can erode the wealth passed on to heirs. Strategies like gifting during your lifetime, establishing trusts, and utilizing exemptions can significantly reduce tax liabilities.

### Family Business Succession Planning

For families with a business, succession **planning is crucial. This involves:**

Identifying potential successors and providing them with training.

Creating a formal transition plan that outlines roles and responsibilities.

Consulting legal and financial advisors to structure the transition effectively.

### 3. Passing Down Values Alongside Wealth

True legacy-building extends beyond financial wealth to include values, ethics, and a vision for how wealth should be used.

### Family Mission Statements

Crafting a family mission statement can provide a framework for how wealth should be managed and used to align with shared values. This could include a commitment to philanthropy, entrepreneurship, or education.

### Encouraging Stewardship

Teach heirs about the responsibilities that come with wealth.

Set clear expectations and guidelines for how inherited assets should be used and managed.

### Part 2: The Role of Philanthropy in Financial Planning

Philanthropy allows individuals and families to use their wealth to make a positive impact on society. By integrating charitable giving into financial planning, you can align your investments with your values while creating a lasting legacy.

### 1. The Benefits of Philanthropy in Legacy-Building

Social Impact: Supporting causes that matter to you helps create a better world for future generations.

**Tax Advantages:** Charitable contributions often come with tax benefits, reducing the overall tax burden.

**Strengthening Family Bonds:** Engaging in philanthropy as a family fosters unity and shared purpose.

**2. Structuring Charitable Giving**

Donor-Advised Funds (DAFs)

DAFs are charitable investment accounts that allow donors to contribute assets, receive an immediate tax deduction, and recommend grants to charities over time.

**Advantages:**

Flexibility in deciding which causes to support.

**The ability to grow contributions tax-free before distributing them.**

**Private Foundations**

Establishing a private foundation allows for greater control over charitable activities and the ability to involve family members in governance.

**Considerations:**

Administrative responsibilities and costs.

Regulatory requirements to maintain tax-exempt status.

**Direct Giving**

This involves donating directly to charities or individuals. While straightforward, it lacks the long-term impact and structure of other philanthropic vehicles.

### 3. Aligning Investments with Values: ESG and Impact Investing

Environmental, Social, and Governance (ESG) investing and impact investing enable you to support causes through your investment portfolio.

**Key Aspects of ESG Investing:**

Investing in companies that prioritize sustainability, ethical labor practices, and strong governance.

Screening out industries that conflict with your values, such as tobacco or fossil fuels.

**Impact Investing:**

Focusing on investments that deliver measurable social or environmental benefits alongside financial returns.

Examples include renewable energy projects, affordable housing, and microfinance initiatives.

### 4. Inspiring the Next Generation to Give

Encouraging younger family members to participate in philanthropic activities can instill a lifelong commitment to giving.

**Ways to Inspire Philanthropy:**

Include children in discussions about charitable causes and decision-making processes.

Create matching programs to amplify their contributions to charitable organizations.

Share stories of how philanthropy has made a difference in others' lives.

Creating a legacy through investing involves more than amassing wealth—it's about intentional planning, empowering the next generation, and making a meaningful impact on society. By focusing on financial literacy, estate planning, and philanthropy, you can ensure that your wealth benefits not only your family but also the world at large.

The process of legacy-building requires vision, discipline, and a long-term commitment to your values. Whether through passing down assets, instilling stewardship, or engaging in philanthropic endeavors, your efforts can leave an indelible mark on future generations and society. With thoughtful planning and action, you can create a legacy that transcends monetary wealth and reflects the principles and priorities that matter most to you.

# Conclusion

## *Your Ultimate Stock Market Playbook in Action*

The journey through the stock market is not a sprint but a marathon—a continuous process of learning, adapting, and growing. This playbook was designed to equip you with the tools, knowledge, and strategies necessary to navigate the complexities of investing and achieve financial success. Now, it's time to put these lessons into action, building a future that reflects both your financial goals and personal values.

### Summary of Key Strategies

Every chapter of this playbook provided critical insights to help you master the art of investing. Let's revisit the essential takeaways that form the foundation of your investment journey:

## *The Foundations of Investing*

Understanding the stock market is the first step toward becoming a confident investor. Knowledge of key terms, market mechanics, and investment vehicles empowers you to make informed decisions.

### Developing a Winning Strategy

Clear financial goals and a well-constructed portfolio are essential. Whether you aim for short-term gains or long-term wealth, aligning your strategy with your objectives ensures a focused and disciplined approach.

### Practical Investing Techniques

From selecting the right brokerage platform to exploring dividend investing, growth strategies, and value opportunities, the techniques outlined in this playbook provide actionable steps for every stage of your investing journey.

### Managing and Growing Your Investments

Successful investing isn't just about making money; it's about protecting and growing it. Regular portfolio monitoring, tax-efficient investing, and risk mitigation strategies ensure sustainability and growth.

### Advanced Strategies

For seasoned investors, advanced techniques like options trading, short selling, and thematic investing open doors to new opportunities. These strategies, when applied with caution and expertise, can enhance returns and diversify income streams.

## Legacy Building and Philanthropy

Investing is more than a financial activity; it's a way to create a lasting legacy. By fostering financial literacy, planning for wealth transfer, and incorporating philanthropy, you can ensure your investments make a meaningful impact on future generations.

## Next Steps for Continued Success

The stock market is ever-evolving, and the most successful investors are those who commit to lifelong learning and adaptability. Here's how you can take the next steps toward continued growth and success:

### 1. Keep Educating Yourself

The financial world is dynamic, with constant changes in market conditions, regulations, and investment trends. Stay informed by:

Reading financial news and publications.

Attending webinars, workshops, or seminars.

Following market analysts and reputable financial experts.

## 2. Review and Refine Your Goals

Your financial goals may change as you progress through different life stages. Regularly revisit your objectives to ensure they align with your current priorities and circumstances.

## 3. Stay Disciplined

Discipline is the cornerstone of successful investing. Resist the urge to react emotionally to market volatility, and stick to your long-term strategy. Remember: patience often leads to greater rewards.

## 4. Leverage Technology and Tools

Modern technology provides investors with an array of tools to simplify and optimize the investing process. Use portfolio trackers, robo-advisors, and analytics platforms to enhance decision-making and efficiency.

## 5. Seek Professional Advice When Needed

While this playbook empowers you with knowledge, there may be situations where professional guidance is invaluable. Financial advisors, tax consultants, and estate planners can help you navigate complex scenarios and optimize outcomes.

**Your Future Awaits**

The stock market is more than a platform for trading shares; it's a gateway to financial freedom and empowerment. As you embark on this journey, remember that every decision you make shapes your financial future. Whether you're investing for retirement, building generational wealth, or funding philanthropic causes, the principles in this playbook will guide you every step of the way.

The ultimate stock market playbook is now in your hands. Use it to make informed choices, seize opportunities, and overcome challenges. Embrace the ups and downs of the market as part of your learning curve, and celebrate each milestone as a testament to your growth.

Success in investing is not measured solely by the wealth you accumulate but by the confidence, resilience, and purpose you develop along the way. You have the knowledge, tools, and strategies—now take action and craft the financial legacy you've always envisioned.

Your journey to mastering the stock market starts now. Take the first step, and let this playbook be your trusted companion as you pave the way to a prosperous and meaningful future.

# Appendices

This section serves as a valuable resource hub to complement the main content of the book. Whether you're a beginner investor seeking guidance or an experienced one looking for advanced tools, the appendices provide actionable insights, curated tools, and essential references to enhance your investing journey.

### A. Stock Market Resources and Tools

To succeed in the stock market, you need access to reliable resources and tools that simplify research, improve decision-making, and provide actionable insights. Below is a list of key resources and tools to elevate your investing game.

**1. Stock Market News Platforms**

Staying updated on the latest market trends and events is critical for informed decision-making. Here are some trusted platforms:

**Bloomberg:** A leading source for real-time financial news, data, and analysis. Bloomberg covers everything from market movements to economic trends.

**CNBC:** Known for its live coverage of stock market events, CNBC provides expert opinions and detailed financial news.

**Market Watch:** This platform focuses on business news, stock analysis, and personal finance tips, catering to a broad audience.

**Yahoo Finance:** A user-friendly platform offering stock market data, earnings reports, and customizable portfolios.

## 2. Stock Screening Tools

Stock screeners help investors filter stocks based on specific criteria such as valuation metrics, sector, or market cap. Popular options include:

**Finviz:** Offers a robust screener with customizable filters and visualization tools to analyze market trends.

**Zacks**: Known for its research on earnings

reports and analyst recommendations, Zacks is ideal for fundamental analysis.

**Morningsta**r: Provides in-depth research on stocks, mutual funds, and ETFs, making it a favorite among long-term investors.

### 3. Portfolio Management Tools

Managing your investments effectively requires tools that track performance, asset allocation, and returns. Some excellent options are:

**Personal Capital:** Combines financial planning with portfolio management, offering detailed insights into your holdings.

Mint: A budgeting app that also tracks your investment performance and net worth.

SigFig: Focuses on portfolio tracking and rebalancing while providing actionable advice.

### 4. Educational Resources

Continuous learning is crucial for any investor. Resources like the following can deepen your knowledge:

**Investopedia:** Offers comprehensive guides, tutorials, and a dictionary for financial and investing terms.

**Khan Academy**: Features free courses on economics, finance, and investing basics.

**Udemy and Coursera**: Both platforms provide affordable online courses, from beginner-level investing to advanced financial modeling.

## B. Frequently Asked Questions (FAQs)

Investors often face common questions and dilemmas when navigating the stock market. Here are answers to frequently asked questions to clarify concepts and improve decision-making.

### *1. How Do I Start Investing in the Stock Market?*

Open a brokerage account with a reputable platform.

Fund your account and identify your financial goals.

Start small, ideally with index funds or ETFs, while learning the basics.

### 2. How Much Money Do I Need to Start Investing?

You can start with as little as $100 on

platforms that offer fractional shares.

Some brokers have no minimum deposit requirements, making it accessible for beginners.

### 3. What Is the Difference Between Stocks and ETFs?

Stocks: Represent ownership in a single company.

ETFs: Are collections of stocks or other securities, offering instant diversification.

### 4. How Do I Know Which Stocks to Buy?

Use stock screeners and fundamental analysis to evaluate companies.

Look for metrics like P/E ratios, dividend yields, and revenue growth.

Diversify across industries to reduce risk.

### 5. What Are Common Mistakes to Avoid?

**Emotional trading:** Avoid panic selling during downturns or buying during hype.

Neglecting diversification: Don't put all your money into a single stock or sector.

Timing the market: Focus on time in the

market rather than trying to predict short-term movements.

### 6. How Do Dividends Work?

Dividends are payments made by companies to their shareholders, usually quarterly.

Reinvesting dividends can compound returns over time, increasing portfolio value.

### 7. What Are the Risks of Margin Trading?

Margin trading amplifies both gains and losses.

You may owe money to your broker if the market moves against you.

It's essential to use leverage responsibly and set stop-loss orders to limit potential losses.

## C. Recommended Reading for Investors

To become a successful investor, you must continually refine your knowledge and skills. The following books and resources are highly recommended for all levels of investors.

### 1. Beginner-Friendly Reads

The Intelligent Investor by Benjamin Graham: A classic that teaches the fundamentals of value investing and risk management.

Common Stocks and Uncommon Profits by Philip Fisher: Focuses on long-term growth investing and identifying quality companies.

### 2. Advanced Investing Books

Security Analysis by Benjamin Graham and David Dodd: A comprehensive guide to evaluating stocks and bonds.

Options, Futures, and Other Derivatives by John Hull: An essential resource for understanding complex financial instruments.

Principles by Ray Dalio: Offers insights into macroeconomic cycles and investment strategies from one of the world's top investors.

### 3. Behavioral Finance and Psychology

Thinking, Fast and Slow by Daniel Kahneman: Explores cognitive biases that affect financial decision-making.

Nudge by Richard H. Thaler and Cass R. Sunstein: Examines how subtle changes in decision-making frameworks can improve financial outcomes.

The Little Book of Behavioral Investing by James Montier: Teaches how to recognize and overcome emotional and psychological traps.

## 4. Economics and Market Trends

**The Wealth of Nations by Adam Smith:** A foundational work on economics and market behavior.

Capital in the Twenty-First Century by Thomas Piketty: Analyzes wealth inequality and its impact on markets.

The Ascent of Money by Niall Ferguson: Provides a historical perspective on the evolution of financial systems and markets.

5. Online Communities and Blogs

Seeking Alpha: A platform where investors share analysis and opinions.

**The Motley Fool:** Offers stock recommendations, educational content, and insights into market trends.

**Financial Samurai:** Focuses on achieving financial independence through investing and smart money management.

This appendix equips you with a comprehensive toolkit to excel in the stock market. The resources, tools, and recommended readings listed here will deepen your knowledge, sharpen your strategies, and guide you toward making informed and profitable decisions. Remember, the key to long-term success is a commitment to continuous learning and disciplined investing. With the right mindset and resources, the stock market can become a powerful ally in your journey toward financial freedom.

www.ingramcontent.com/pod-product-compliance
Lightning Source LLC
Chambersburg PA
CBHW052148220526
45471CB00004B/1572